T0063440

GIVE
RECEIVE
IMPROVE

Books by Salwana Ali

A Handbook for First Time Managers—Critical Pointers That New
Managers Need to Know to Succeed in Their Managerial Role

Give Receive Improve—A New Manager's Guide
to Feedback and Improvement
(With Lisa Lam)

Skill Sets for New Managers Series

GIVE
RECEIVE
IMPROVE

A New Manager's Guide to Feedback and Improvement

SALWANA ALI AND LISA LAM

PARTRIDGE
A Penguin Random House Company

To order additional copies of this book, contact
Toll Free 800 101 2657 (Singapore)
Toll Free 1 800 81 7340 (Malaysia)
orders.singapore@partridgepublishing.com

www.partridgepublishing.com/singapore

CONTENTS

Special dedication to all first time managers and new managers

Preface

I published a book entitled A Handbook for First Time Managers in the first quarter of 2013 which is a practical guide for first time managers to prepare for their managerial role. Since then, I have received feedback from various clients and readers suggesting that I should offer guidance to other types of behavioural skills for first time managers and new managers.

Responding to these feedbacks, I decided to establish the 'Skill Sets for New Managers Series' practical guides. 'Give, Receive, Improve: A New Manager's Guide to Feedback and Improvement' is the first book under these series.

When the idea to write this book came up, I recalled some significant events during my time, working in the corporate world. I spent half of my corporate experience in Microsoft (a subsidiary in Malaysia), where I learned the most. I gained exposure to many situations that hinged around 'feedback for continuous improvement', ranging from candid observational feedback to formal business processes utilizing feedback as the tool to improve performance.

Going down this memory lane, one individual, Lisa Lam, who happened to join Microsoft in the same week I did, stood out. In a way, we 'grew up' together during our early years in Microsoft. We went through the same experience learning about the culture that placed a huge emphasis on 'feedback for continuous improvement'.

I invited Lisa Lam to write this book together with me. I believe her experience in her later part of her career with Microsoft, working in multiple locations with multiple cultures will add rich dimensions to this book.

Give, Receive, Improve: A New Manager Guide to Feedback and Improvement will benefit first time managers and new managers immensely. It provides comprehensive guidance on how to give and receive feedback effectively and how to move forward with the feedback received.

First time managers and new managers will acquire key approaches in honing their skills in giving and receiving feedback. We practically segregated the components of giving and receiving feedback as each process is unique and calls for different approaches and mind-sets while performing them.

The key learning that we would like first time managers and new managers to acquire is that **feedback is powerful**. As a matter of fact, feedback is the best tool and it comes in handy for them to continuously improve themselves, as individuals and as managers. Their ability to effectively give, receive and do something significant about feedback will help them in developing high performing teams which in turn will benefit the organisation as a whole.

In addition, we presented numerous examples of feedback processes currently utilized in typical organisations settings. First time managers and new managers can learn from these examples. They can apply the recommended approach to hone their skills in giving and receiving feedback through each example provided.

In developing this book, Lisa and I went through these critical questions:

- What do first time managers and new managers need to know about feedback?
- How do they prepare themselves to give and receive feedback effectively?
- Where does continuous improvement come from?

- How can they improve in giving and receiving feedback?
- Is there a way of monitoring progress and improvement in their skills of giving and receiving feedback?

We recalled our experiences for each question. While giving, receiving and acting on feedback is more of an 'art-form', we strived to compartmentalise and inject some form of 'science' to the whole process. Such approach enabled us to clearly provide methodical steps on how to give, receive and act on feedback.

First time and new managers can easily follow the steps and practice the correct way of giving, receiving and acting on feedback.

Salwana Ali
Kuala Lumpur, Malaysia

Lisa Lam
Adelaide, Australia

Acknowledgements

We would like to especially acknowledge and thank Dato' Dr Faridah Ismail and Janet Khoo for taking time to help us read, edit and provide feedback to us.

We would like to also thank many of our friends and primary readers for their support and encouragement when we had to bounce ideas, challenge the basis of the book as well as the value add that we would provide to you, the new manager.

The journey of writing this book was filled with giving, receiving and improving upon our ideas and content, so rest assured we know exactly how it feels to be on all ends of feedback.

The journey is well worth the ride.

Introduction

"Feedback is the breakfast of champions"
—Ken Blanchard

Tiger Woods, Roger Federer and Usain Bolt. They are in a class of their own.

They make very difficult things look easy.

They are the world champions.

What are the common attributes of these champions?

Champions practice hard to achieve excellence.

Tiger Woods trains 8 hours every day (when he doesn't participate in golf tournaments), combining cardio, weight and core/flexibility training with his golf practice routine. The core training components are described below:

- One hour of cardio training in the early morning comprises of either bicycling, a 7 mile endurance run or 3 mile speed run[1].

---

[1]   Brent Kelley, posted on About.com Golf, "What is Tiger Woods' Workout Routine?" *About.com Blog,* http://golf.about.com/od/tigerwoods/f/tiger-woods-workout.htm

- One hour of weight training, lifting 60 to 70 percent of his normal weights and focusing on a lot of reps and different sets[2].
- Golf practice routine comprises of the following[3]:

  o Two hours of range-work and on-course swing work, followed by 30 minutes to an hour of putting practice.
  o Plays nine holes.
  o Another 3-4 hours of on-course work focusing on the swing and short game. Sometimes, it includes another nine holes of playing golf.

- 30 minute lifting weights to work on his upper body strength[4].

Tiger Woods treats his fitness as a long term strategy to be the best in the field as stated, "I view fitness as a long-term strategy for building and maintaining endurance, strength and agility. It's a continuous cycle of training and recovery."[5]

Champions thrive on continuous assessment.

The champion's way of life is about dealing with the pressures of expectations. On any given day, the public, sports pundits, the media and

---

[2] Brent Kelley, posted on About.com Golf, "What is Tiger Woods' Workout Routine?" *About.com Blog,* http://golf.about.com/od/tigerwoods/f/tiger-woods-workout.htm

[3] Brent Kelley, posted on About.com Golf, "How Much Does Tiger Woods Practice Golf?" *About.com Blog,* http://golf.about.com/od/tigerwoods/f/tiger-woods-practice.htm

[4] Brent Kelley, posted on About.com Golf, "How Much Does Tiger Woods Practice Golf?" *About.com Blog,* http://golf.about.com/od/tigerwoods/f/tiger-woods-practice.htm

[5] Brent Kelley, posted on About.com Golf, "How Much Does Tiger Woods Practice Golf?" *About.com Blog,* http://golf.about.com/od/tigerwoods/f/tiger-woods-practice.htm

many other groups of stakeholders expect them to be at their best. They are constantly being assessed: Both direct and indirect assessment.

Direct assessment is the feedback from their coaches and managers. After every tennis game, there are numerous statistical data that Roger Federer and his coach would be looking at. First serve percentage, second serve percentage, number of winners, number of unforced errors, number of breaks converted, number of winners at the net and many others. Analysis of these data would help them in determining what is working, what is not and what they should be doing differently in the next game. As a matter of fact, the overall analysis would help them in strategising every unique game with a unique player. For instance, Federer would have a specific strategy on how to beat Nadal by reviewing all the previous data that he had playing Nadal many times before. Based on these analyses, Federer would be able to plan on the type of training that he should be focusing on prior to each game.

Indirect assessment is any form of general feedback. A headline on a newspaper, for example, is also a category of feedback. The latest example of a general feedback on Woods' quote of "Winning takes care of everything" upon his comeback to world number 1 rank has mixed responses from the public[6]. Some criticised Nike for such a headline suggesting that it conveyed a negative message on the backdrop of his infidelity acts three years ago. In fact, the past three years, Woods received much indirect negative feedback and he had struggled in his game, not winning any titles during the three year duration. Despite all the challenging hardships, Woods kept on working and grinding hard to get back to his best. Finally, just 3 months into 2013, he has won three key tournaments; Farmers Insurance Open, WGC Cadillac Championship and Arnold Palmer Invitational.

Undoubtedly, he has thrived on continuous assessment very well.

---

[6]   Lynn Zinser, "Pushback on Nike Ad Celebrating Woods," *The New York Times*, March 26th, 2013, accessed November 11th, 2013.

Champions take feedback / assessment positively to further improve their performance.

Regardless of the types of feedback, champions know how to deal with both positive and negative feedback.

The underlying principle that they adopt is to take feedback as a method of improving themselves, physically and mentally. They condition themselves to be critical about their own performances. They always search for ways to add a competitive advantage. They listen to feedback or assessment with an open mind, conditionally ready to embrace the suggestions and recommendations for further improvement when such feedback or assessments are rightfully applicable to their situations.

Usain Bolt clocked 10.04 seconds in Ostrava in May 2012. He was heavily criticised for failing to break the 10 seconds in a final since 2009. He took the criticism graciously and said, "I explained to my coach that my legs were not feeling that energetic, probably through a lack of sleep and not enough food. You never have a good race every time you run. You have to just put that behind you and move on. It's not a worry. I have a lot more races and the main one is at the Olympics. I have set a high standard for myself so I know people like to see me run fast. I can't look at it as pressure. People expect you to do certain things—I know I will have my bad races but I have to stay strong and focused. I never stress over things like this. I have gone through so much, so many things that even if I lose every race up to the Olympics it doesn't matter because I know that I have one focus and that is just to go to the Olympics and do great things."[7]

True to what he said, Bolt won the 100m, 200m and 4x100m in the 2012 Olympic Games.

---

[7] Sportsmail Reporter, "Need more chicken nuggets, Usain? Bolt claims lack of food led to slow race," *MailOnline*, May 29th, 2012, accessed November 11th, 2013. http://www.dailymail.co.uk/sport/othersports/article-2151574/Usain-Bolt-claims-lack-food-blame-slow-run.html

He was mentally strong to take such hard assessment or criticism. He did not waver. He was sure of his focus and knew exactly where he stood. He proved it by his excellent performance in the Olympic Games, fulfilling every stakeholder's expectations.

The key lesson from the champions is that there is no short cut. You have to be focused (almost single minded), put in all the hours to master your trade, readily accept feedback and/or assessment and proactively take actions on that feedback to continuously improve yourself.

Continuous improvement through intensive practice and assessment breeds excellent performance as modelled in the PAI (Practice, Assess, Improve) Ladder below:

The PAI (Practice, Assess, Improve) Ladder

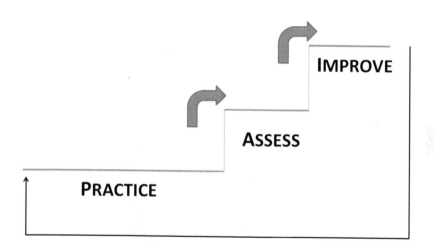

The Practice, Assess and Improve (PAI) model is a reiterative process of continuous improvement. Three key tasks that you need to do continuously are:

- Practice: Doing the same thing repeatedly on a daily basis.
- Assess: Observe, engage and capture areas of improvement.
- Improve: Execute specific action plans as required.

You can be a champion in your own field by adopting the PAI model, adapted from the champion's best practice.

A quick scenario to demonstrate the PAI model, as depicted in Scenario 1 below:

Scenario 1: Demonstrating the PAI Model

Sarah is a telemarketer with Pivotal Telemarketing Services Limited (PTSL), a telemarketing outsourcing company. PTSL assists its clients to sell their services such as technical support, training services and many others to their respective prospects on the phone. One of Sarah's major tasks is to call the list of prospects that her clients have, explain about the service offerings and get an agreement for the client to move to the next stage of the sales cycle. For example, if it is a training service, that could be an agreement to attend the training. If it is a technical support service, that could be an agreement to meet and have a discussion with a sales executive to explore further on the suitable solution for their respective organisations.

Sarah knows that she needs to work on her persuasive communication on the phone to perfection in order to enhance her success rate in converting her prospects to the next stage of the sales cycle. For this purpose, she adopts the PAI model of continuous improvement that consists of these components:

- *__Practice:__ She develops her script for the phone call. She rehearses the conversation out loud to hear exactly how she sounds. She records her conversations. She does this repetitively, rehearsing the script until she feels that her conversation flows naturally.*
- *__Assess:__ At every hour interval, she takes 15 minutes break just to listen to the recording of her conversations with the prospects. She takes note on what's working and what's not. She then lists down key action items that she needs to improve on. She rewrites some of the scripts to remind herself of the new changes that she wants to implement.*

- *Improve: After the 15 minute break, she continues her phone calls. She communicates to the prospects executing key improvement that she has captured into her conversation, as she sees fit. She continues doing this until the next interval hour, at which time; she starts the assessment process again.*

Sarah goes through the same routine every day. She finds this approach very effective as her conversion rate increases dramatically over time. In the past three months, she has improved her conversion ratio from 2:15 to 3:10.

Like Woods, Federer and Bolt, Sarah demonstrated that she can achieve the targeted outcomes using the same approach adopted by champions—practice, assess and improve; done in repetitive manner.

You can also do the same.

You can unleash the power of feedback for continuous improvement.

How to Use This Book?

This book is divided into five main sections as listed below:

- Section 1: What and Why?
- Section 2: Giving and Receiving Feedback.
- Section 3: Different Types of Feedback.
- Section 4: Mastering Feedback Skills for Continuous Improvement.
- Section 5: Moving Forward.

Section 1: What and Why explains what feedback is and why you should care about feedback. The main purpose of these two chapters within this section is to establish a common understanding about feedback and its benefits.

Section 2: Giving and Receiving Feedback consists of two chapters on how to give and receive feedback. You will understand the objectives of feedback in reinforcing good behaviours and rectifying bad behaviours. You will acquire clear guiding principles on giving and receiving feedback. You will learn the key steps in preparing to give and receive feedback. In addition, you will recognise the options on what to do with feedback.

Section 3: Different Types of Feedback consists of two chapters on Internal Feedback and External Feedback. The main objective of this section is to guide you on how to leverage the different types of feedback available to you. The most common types of internal feedback that organisations typically utilize will provide you the understanding on the feedback objectives and how you can achieve the most impact from the feedback. In terms of external feedback, the key learning will be how best to utilize the survey results to ensure you achieve significant improvement from your current situation.

Section 4: Mastering Feedback Skills for Continuous Improvement consists of two chapters namely, Power of Feedback for Continuous Improvement and Honing Your Skills.

Power of Feedback for Continuous Improvement details out five key scenarios on how organisations use feedback as a tool for improvement in their standard business processes such as business review, performance goal setting, customer service, project monitoring and employee engagement.

Honing Your Skills is about guiding you in building your capabilities to give and receive feedback effectively within the setting of your standard business processes. You will learn from the specific examples provided. In fact, you can practice the approach and apply it in your real life organisational settings as well.

Section 5: Moving Forward consists of two chapters, namely, So What's Next and Feedback Toolkit.

So What's Next ensures that you will take action based on what you have learned in giving and receiving feedback. You can follow the recommendations in this chapter to make sure that the new habit of giving and receiving feedback is developed.

Feedback Toolkit describes an approach that you can take moving forward to inculcate the habit of giving and receiving feedback. The feedback toolkit is a buddy system that directs you in the right manner to achieve your goal in improving your skills to give and receive feedback effectively. It helps you to manage and assess your skills in giving and receiving feedback. Over time, with practice, giving and receiving feedback will become a habit to you.

We recommend 'fresh' first time managers and new managers to read this book in the current sequence of arrangement.

For those who are familiar with feedback and its processes, you can choose to proceed to specific chapters that are relevant to you. For instance, if you wish to improve your skills in giving and receiving feedback in a specific setting of a business process of an organisation, you can proceed to Chapter 8—Honing Your Skills.

Let us enjoy this journey in learning what feedback is all about and how to unleash the power of feedback for continuous improvement.

SECTION 1:

What and Why?

1 What is Feedback?

"A Truthful Evaluation of Yourself Gives Feedback for Growth and Success."
—*Brenda Johnson Padgitt*

According to Peter F. Drucker in his book People and Performance, "Managers are the basic resource of the business enterprise." And therefore it is critical to ensure that managers are well equipped to manage, lead and develop their teams for the success of the organisation. One of the skills required to achieve that is the ability to communicate clearly and constructively to both management and their teams in the form of effective feedback.

Feedback in the workplace is about "the flow of information among associates, usually as an evaluation of a project or work completed and the sharing of observations about job performance or work-related behaviours."[8]

Feedback is almost surely seen as something that is scary and negative, most probably because we have had bad feedback experiences in the past. Who can ever say that they had never experienced a negative feedback and felt awful after that? And it is therefore no coincidence that with the slightest mention of the word "feedback", our response is either to defend or to attack.

---

[8]   Harris, Jamie O. Giving Feedback (Harvard Business School Press, 2006), 4.

The irony of feedback is that we are both givers and receivers of feedback on a continuous basis. Whether we realise it or not, we are in a constant state of giving feedback to each other. We do it both consciously and unconsciously in both casual and formal settings. We do it to create an outcome that we want, whether good or bad. In most cases, everyone who gives and receives feedback wants a positive outcome of continuous improvement.

Here are some casual examples of feedback that we give without the slightest effort.

Everyday casual feedback:

- "You look great today!"
- "You look a little serious today."
- "You look stressed."
- "You lost some weight, did you?"

In the workplace, examples of feedback can range from simple congratulatory to negative ones such as:

- "Good job on the presentation to the management team."
- "You can do better . . ."
- "You will need to consider another career path!"

I think that equally important is to highlight what **Feedback is NOT** and in the book Giving Feedback by Harvard Business School Press, "feedback is **not** a form of punishment and to keep in mind that feedback is not necessarily negative, not a one-way monologue, does not need to be a wrestling match, is not an opportunity for a personal attack and does not represent the only point of view."[9].

The start of giving any feedback lies with the purpose or intention of the feedback. **The purpose of feedback is to either reinforce or rectify**

---

[9]   Harris, Jamie O. Giving Feedback (Harvard Business School Press, 2006), 5.

an observed behaviour. The observed behaviour can be derived from what we see and what we hear along with any other forms of information e.g. goals, metrics and survey results. Upon evaluating the various forms of information, the feedback will then be developed and delivered.

In summary, this is how I think about feedback:

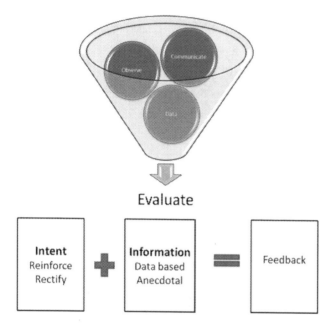

There are many different kinds of feedback ranging from casual to formal or professional feedback. In each situation, how each of us provides and receives feedback is critical in the quality of the interaction and relationship that we have with one another. There are a number of components that must exist in order for us to give and receive feedback positively.

Critical components to effective feedback:

- **Trust:** Is there a relationship based on trust? Both the giver and receiver must have a certain level of trust. Without a level of trust from both sides, there will not be an honest and open dialogue.

29

- **Understanding**: Is there a perceived level of understanding for the given situation? The level of understanding will determine the level of relevance in the feedback.
- **Credibility**: Is there a level of credibility in the giver of the feedback? The perceived level of credibility will determine the level of acceptance to the feedback.

As an example, I would like to improve on my golf swing. I have a friend who plays golf. She gives me advice on how to improve my golf swing. Do I accept her feedback or not? I trust my friend and know that she understands my situation but I don't find her to be a credible golfer hence I might not accept her feedback.

2 Why Should I Care About Feedback?

"No Feedback, No Motivation"

—*Kevin McManus*

Most of us, me included, would love to be able to take feedback and just magically improve and be better the next minute. On the other side of it we would also like to be like "Teflon" where nothing sticks and therefore no bruised egos to handle. However, as with everything in life, that is not the case. In fact regardless of whether we ask for feedback or not, we will receive feedback from people and situations around us. It is no longer a question of whether we should care or not about feedback but more of *what we should do with feedback* and how we can use it *positively* to improve.

From the time each of us is born, feedback is part and parcel of our lives. Imagine a baby, entering this world and what is the feedback that he or she receives? Feedback ranges from what the senses can pick up e.g. lights around them, sounds that are heard and the soothing touch of a parent. The baby does not only receive feedback but can also give very effective feedback to adults in the form of loud wailing when hunger is at the top of the mind or when a change of clean diaper is needed.

As we grow up and become toddlers, we are encouraged to crawl with words like "come on, you can make it", "a little more" and when we reach the goal or destination, a reward is given, usually the toy that we were after and a great big smile from a parent for arriving at the destination. In many ways, we are still the same. When we achieve a goal or a certain destination, we expect some form of a reward or a moment to be proud of our accomplishments. Those feelings and expectations never go away.

From those little moments to every time when we do something whether good or bad, we receive a reaction whether in words of encouragement, as simple as "you did it" or "good work" or "I am proud of you" and on the flip side negative words such as "you are no good" or "that's very naughty", all these moments of feedback provide building blocks to our character. This will determine how we react and respond to the people and circumstances around us.

Now let's turn our attention to the workplace and as a new manager.

A big milestone in anyone's career is when one is promoted to be a manager. Each of us starts out as an idealist when we first become a manager. After the initial euphoria of reaching a milestone or goal in your career, you will realise that the responsibility of others are on your shoulders. It is with this new sense of purpose that will drive you to the need to further improve. In order to improve, a key tool in your manager's toolkit is feedback. What, When and How to use feedback will be important.

In fact, it will be very clear that the very first form of "feedback" that you will receive from your team will not be verbal in nature but in the form of changes in body language and whispers in the corridor. Now, you are the topic of conversation. The fact is, being a manager for the first time is extremely scary but you are not alone.

Now when I look back, I can laugh at myself as I can clearly remember being excited, happy and full of self-created expectations of how I could make changes and have a great team and be impactful. However, that was the furthest from the truth. When I looked at the team that I was going to manage, a sudden sense of dread and "what in the world did I get myself into?" fear struck me. I was no different from them, not any smarter and certainly not better and how would I be able to help them were the biggest questions I had every day. To add to my own insecurities and fears, somehow the number of people giving me feedback exponentially grew ranging from how bad the team was to how great it was and to top it off, they were giving me feedback independently of me asking for it.

I have to say, what did save me, was attending Steven Covey's 7 Habits of Highly Effective People which basically helped me to seek first to understand and the concept of sharpening the saw. I came to realise that whether I wanted it or not, I was going to receive feedback, so why not make full use of it by seeking to understand not just the content of the feedback but the intent of the person giving it and look for ways to improve upon the areas that are weak. I have of course over a long period of time learned to enjoy the feedback process (not necessarily the feedback itself).

The responsibility of what we do with feedback rests solely on our shoulders. We can decide to respond in the following ways:

- Defend
- Deny
- Reflect and Assess
- Accept and Improve

How we view feedback is the key to unlocking the power of it in order for us to improve. It is therefore important that we learn some simple framework and tips on giving, receiving and making the necessary changes from the feedback that we receive.

Feedback should be viewed as a critical tool to propel you forward and not to hold you back. The worst position to be in is to remain stagnant. Therefore, seize the opportunity to give feedback to encourage others to improve and seek feedback to improve your own skills.

SECTION 2:

Giving and Receiving Feedback

3 Giving Feedback

"If your intention in giving someone feedback is to judge or criticize, you'll fail to inspire a shift in their behavior."

—*Misti Burmeister*

There are in essence two forms of feedback which we have called Active and Passive.

Active feedback is one where the feedback is given and received *instantaneously* or *in real time* and usually in a discussion setting. Passive feedback on the other hand requires time to gather the information usually through surveys and in a wider context upon which the feedback is then given.

Therefore the differences between "Active" and "Passive" feedback are the length of time between giving and receiving feedback as well as the usage of the information or content for feedback.

Active Feedback

Active feedback means a direct mode of giving and receiving feedback. The process of giving and receiving feedback happens instantaneously and the feedback recipient can mutually decide with the person who gives the feedback, on specific action items as the next steps and how best to measure and/or monitor the desired improvement.

The **purposes** of feedback are:

- To **reinforce** good behaviours.
- To **rectify** bad behaviours.

These guiding principles will help you provide effective feedback:

- **When giving feedback:**

  o **Begin with the positive:** People need encouragement. It is imperative that you recognise what they have done well first. This will make it easier for them to appreciate the objectivity of your feedback. Hearing the positive first would also increase the likelihood of them to take the negatives in a respectful manner.

  o **Describe specific behaviours that can be changed:** Avoid making general and categorical statements about behaviour. For instance, 'you are being rude' doesn't help them in understanding what exactly that they did wrong. A statement such as 'I observe that you screamed at the attendee when he asked question . . . .' describes a precise behaviour which offers a real opportunity for them to learn and fix.

  o **Adopt descriptive rather than evaluative mode:** Always describe behaviour or specific actions such as "I observe you have shown up late in a few important meetings recently" rather than "I observe you appear not interested anymore . . . ."

  o **Offer alternatives:** Seek understanding from them on what they could have done differently. Let them come up with specific actions. In the event that they struggle to come up with specific actions, then offer some suggestions.

o **Own the feedback:** You have to take responsibility of the feedback that you offer. Instead of saying to the other person, "You are . . . .", which implies a universal agreement of opinion about the person, begin with "I think . . ." or "I feel . . . .". This reflects that you are taking responsibility of the feedback and not simply giving a general opinion which you don't own.

o **Leave the recipient with a choice:** End a feedback on a clear choice of actions that they can act upon. They would have enough information to gauge on whether or not they want to make such changes and the final decision is entirely up to them.

I like to have this in my mind as part of my way of preparing to give feedback, "**give the feedback like how I would want the feedback to be given to me**". I believe that once we have the right frame of mind and intention of giving the feedback, we will be able to give authentic, concise, specific and timely feedback that aims for positive influence and impact.

We are all aware of the impact of feedback both good and bad ones and yet, we all at one time or another make the mistake of giving ineffective feedback. Some aspects of ineffective feedback are:

- **General or Generic.** Feedback that is generic in nature does not help to reinforce or rectify behaviour. As an example, "Good work, well done." What was good? Can you improve on that? Don't know or it's unclear. It would be better to say "Good work on the product presentation which was clear and articulate . . ." This would indicate that it was on the presentation and presentation skill.

- **Negative or Accusatory.** Feedback that is negative or accusatory in nature will almost always lead to a defensive position and not a positive outcome. As an example, "It is your fault that we lost the sales deal." What is the outcome of such a feedback? It would be better to say "We have lost the sales deal and now let's think about how we can secure the others." Both deals with the loss of the sales deal but one is negative and blame centred while the other is taking joint accountability and to work on a positive outcome.

- **Timeliness.** Feedback given at an inappropriate time will lose its impact. This will happen even if the feedback itself is positive. As an example, "The presentation with customer ABC was excellent and you connected very well with the audience." However, this presentation took place 3 months ago. For most people, we would have forgotten what happened last week let alone 3 months ago.

Feedback on performance is extremely sensitive and daunting for any first time managers and in fact for all managers despite age and experience. This is because if handled correctly it is an extremely powerful tool to motivate and develop an individual. While on the flipside, it can be demotivating and can create a sense of distrust and confusion which will not only lead the individual down the wrong path but potentially the entire team.

In the **Coaching and Mentoring for Dummies book by Marty Broustein**, he outlines that "performance feedback can be given two ways: through constructive feedback or through praise and criticism. Don't fall into the trap of giving praise and criticism on employee performance." As praise and criticism are both personal judgments and the information given is general and vague, it is therefore essential that we learn how to give constructive feedback.

Now let's explore the steps to giving feedback.

Steps To Giving Feedback

There are basically 3 key steps to perform in order to prepare to give feedback and they are:

- Gathering Information
- Evaluating the information that has been collected
- Giving the Feedback

Step 1: Gathering Information

The starting point is always to gather information. Information can be gathered through various sources such as:

- **Observations**: We observe how individuals behave, react in group dynamics, interact with people, demonstrate leadership attributes and so on. It is a powerful tool that each of us has in our arsenal to determine whether a behaviour should be encouraged or discouraged.
- **Communication:** We learn the depth of knowledge and experience through what is **communicated**. We can also learn what touches a person's heart and how passionate someone is based on how the words are delivered.
- **Data:** Based on performance based data or facts; it is how objectives and performance goals are measured to demonstrate effectiveness of the individual in a role.

Step 2: Evaluate the Information Gathered

At this stage, there is a need to evaluate which information should be filtered down to what are valuable and necessary for feedback to improve performance.

There is usually a lot of information that is gathered which are not necessary or critical for feedback hence the ability to decide what is important and what is not is crucial.

A good starting point is to evaluate whether the behaviour is cohesive and positive in building teams or destructive and negative. If it is positive, then the question is whether it can be harnessed and improved upon and if it is negative, how to ensure that it does not continue. If the behaviour does not impact work related performance, then it is not critical in your manager's feedback.

Step 3: Giving the Feedback

At this stage, plan to give the feedback with these key elements:

- Purpose of the feedback
- Relevant content
- 'Fit-to-Purpose' approach
- Preparation on how to conduct the feedback session

Let us take a detailed view of all the four elements in planning to give feedback.

Purpose of the Feedback

The purpose of any feedback should be to motivate positive change and improvement and never to tear someone down. Hence, always be clear on whether the feedback is to **reinforce or rectify behaviour**.

Relevant Content

In order for feedback to achieve its purpose it needs to be:

- **Specific**: The feedback must be on a specific action or observation. This will ensure that it's very clear to the receiver of the feedback on what needs to be addressed.
- **Significance**: The significance of the behaviour or issue as it relates to the effects on you or those around you.
- **Seek to Understand**: Seek to understand the reason for the specific action or behaviour will make the discussion a collaborative effort vs. a directive.

- **Suggest an alternative solution or to help:** This helps to demonstrate that you have taken time to think about the feedback and to "own" the challenge just as much as the person.

> **Content should have the 4 S:**
> **Specific, Significance, Seek, Suggest**

'Fit-to-Purpose' Approach

'Fit-to-Purpose' approach is critical to provide comfort and 'safety-net' to the receivers of feedback. The receiver must feel that the giver of feedback is genuinely interested and care about them. Such comfort and sense of security can be achieved with the presence of these 3 components:

- **Timing and frequency**

   o **As soon as possible: The** most effective feedback should take place as close as possible to the time the action or observation is made so that it is fresh in the minds of both the giver and the receiver of the feedback. This makes the conversation relevant and powerful.

   o **Regular and Consistent:** It is important to maintain a regular and consistent formal discussion with your employees to ensure that a rhythm is established where work can be reviewed and feedback given on specific campaigns or skills or overall work accomplishments. This is a more formal setting but a necessary one to ensure that the communication lines are open to both the manager and the employee as we all know just how busy the day can get.

- **Appropriate environment.**

  o The environment plays a part in the overall experience. As an example, a manager would not give work performance feedback in a bar.

- **Communication method**

  o **Face to Face.** Having regular one on one with your direct report or manager.

  o **Non Face to Face.** Written communication methods such as letters and emails are some common examples.

Preparation on How to Conduct the Feedback Session

Preparation is critical to ensure that the feedback experience is positive for both the giver and the receiver.

Two key steps in preparing how to conduct the feedback session are:

- Ensure that the information presented is valid.
- Adopt the appropriate behaviour of active engagement in a positive manner.

Let us explore the application of the above steps in the feedback example below:

John, I noticed that you managed to <u>captivate your audience with relevant data points</u> that really <u>convinced me that the product that you were promoting is good.</u> <u>What I would like to know is</u> the use of the last data point which was against a competitor. It made me feel uncomfortable. <u>What I might suggest is to focus</u> on the product's benefits and not on the competition

---

The above example presents:

- The validity of the information as it does the following:

  o Highlights specific observation
  o Demonstrates how the feedback relates to the giver of the feedback
  o Seeks to understand the context or action
  o Makes a recommendation to the person to ensure that the feedback is both complete and actionable.

- Adoption of the appropriate behaviour of active engagement in a positive manner:

  o The intonation that the giver of the feedback used sounds positive acknowledging specifically what went well, what he or she was not comfortable about and a suggestion on what needs to be done differently.

There have been many examples where even with the best of intentions feedback can be taken very negatively and instead of desired positive response, extremely negative response is the outcome. Therefore let us consider these following examples and identify areas where we could improve upon.

Example 1:

After a successful launch of a marketing campaign, with over 3,000 people attending and 30% response with interest to purchase, the manager comes up to the marketing executive and says the following:

Manager: "That was a great launch and you have put in a great amount of effort and it's great that the feedback from customers has been positive."

Executive: "Thanks boss and without the team and your support, it would not have been positive."

Manager: "Yeah, but I had hoped that you could have had more than 30% response rate. Our last launch had over 40%."

Question: What was the intention of the manager?

Manager sees a great potential in this Executive and would like to motivate him further and ensure that he aims higher.

Question: What do you think would be the response of the Executive to the Manager's feedback?

Response A: I will aim to do better next time, if there is a next time.

Response B: I can never satisfy the manager so why even bother.

Response C: Try and justify my situation so that the manager can see why this event is different and that 30% response rate is great.

Question: Did the feedback from the Manager achieve the desired outcome?

Whether the desired outcome is achieved or not depends on a number of factors as listed earlier. Let us takes a deeper look at them.

1. **Purpose of feedback:**

   - The purpose of feedback is either to reinforce good behaviour or to rectify bad behaviour.
   - In the above example, it is not clear whether the manager wants to reinforce good behaviour or rectify bad behaviour.

2. **Relevancy of Content:**

- **Specific**: Was the feedback specific? In this example, the feedback was general about the event and not specific about any behaviour or actions of the executive. A specific feedback could be "It was a great launch and *your ability to bring everyone together and organise the event demonstrates your leadership abilities.*" This would have indicated a specific skill that the executive demonstrated which the manager observed and wanted to reinforce.

- **Significance:** Did the manager relate the feedback that was given? The manager missed the opportunity and it could have been a simple sentence as *"This demonstrated to me that you are capable of managing and leading bigger marketing campaigns."*

- **Seek to Understand**: The manager did not seek to understand further or open the discussion. The manager should have just said *"I am curious about how you thought the launch went.*

- **Suggestion:** The manager did make a recommendation around the response rate but because the initial conversation was not crafted well, the recommendation did not achieve its desired impact. The manager could have said *"I would recommend that in future, we attract the right target audience in order to achieve a higher response rate."*

3. **'Fit-to-Purpose' Approach:**

- **Timing:** As feedback should be specific, the timing of the feedback is critical and in this example, the feedback was timely as it was after the event and not 2 weeks after the event.

- **How the feedback was communicated:** In this example, it would appear to be rather informal and therefore would cause doubt to the Executive as to what is the best way to handle this feedback.

- **Environment:** Where the feedback was given and taken plays a part in the formality as well as seriousness of the feedback. In this example, it would seem that the feedback was at the location of the launch and just after the event and therefore may not have been an appropriate place for formal feedback.

4. Preparation on How to Conduct the Feedback Session

- **Ensure the information presented is valid:** In the above example, there was surely a lot of information presented. However, there was no evidence to support the validity of the information. For instance, the receiver of the feedback would be struggling to figure out what the positive feedback from the customers meant. Was it the product presentation or the ambience of the launch site?
- **Adopt the appropriate behaviour of active engagement in a positive manner:** The manager in the above example, tried to sound positive. However, it was not clear that he meant what he said as he ended the conversation with a negative remark without any appropriate suggestions or recommendations.

Example 2

Performance review conducted over the phone.

Manager: As you know I am very busy and this is the only time that I have to give you the results of your performance review.

Executive: Oh I see. Ok.

Manager: Good. Over the course of the last year, you have exceeded all your goals and expectations and it has been a pleasure to have you in the team and the feedbacks from your team mates have been positive. So congratulations.

Executive: That's great to hear and know.

Manager: If there are no questions, I will let you go about your day and
            see you when I am back in the office.
Executive: Sure. Thanks.

Question: *What was the intention of the manager?*

Manager thought that because the overall review was good and positive about the executive, he could just give a quick summary of the review over the phone and pick up the conversation later. No harm done since it was a positive review for the executive.

Question: *What do you think would be the response of the Executive to the Manager's feedback?*

Response A: Is this for real?
Response B: That's great. Everything must be great and no areas of improvement or challenges. Let's continue doing what I have been doing.
Response C: That's great but what should I do next? No areas of improvement? I know some things didn't turn out well, so what now?

Question: *Did the feedback from the Manager achieve the desired outcome?*

Whether the desired outcome is achieved or not depends on a number of factors as listed earlier. Let us take a deeper look at them.

1. Purpose of Feedback:

- The purpose of feedback is either to reinforce good behaviour or to rectify bad behaviour.

- In the above example, it is not clear whether the manager wants to reinforce good behaviour or rectify bad behaviour.

2. Relevancy of Content:

- **Specific**: Was the feedback specific? In this example, the feedback was general and did not offer any areas that the Executive did well or needed improvements.
- **Significance:** Did the manager relate the feedback that was given? The manager only provided an insight that *"it has been a pleasure to have you in the team and the feedbacks from your team mates have been positive."* Could the manager have provided more? The manager could have said *"Your performance has demonstrated to me that you are able to organise and manage complexities and that makes me comfortable to give to you more responsibilities."*
- **Seek to Understand**: The manager did not seek to understand further or open the discussion. The manager should have just said *"I am curious about how you thought your performance went.*
- **Suggestion:** The manager did not make any suggestions for further improvements. The manager could have said *"I would recommend that you look into improving your project management skills through attending a course."*

3. 'Fit-to-Purpose' Approach:

- **Timing**: Ad-hoc feedback around performance review is never good even if the result of the review is good. It should be conducted in the time frame which is called for.
- **How the feedback was communicated**: In this example, it would appear to be rather informal and therefore would cause more questions and doubts than giving the executive a good positive feeling that everything did go as well as what the manager had claimed.

- **Environment**: Giving performance review feedback over the phone is clearly not the appropriate medium or place for such an important conversation and yet I am certain, we have each encountered something similar to this in the past.

4. **Preparation on How to Conduct the Feedback Session**

- **Ensure the information presented is valid:** In the above example, there was surely a lot of information presented. However, there was no evidence to support the validity of the information. For instance, the receiver of the feedback would be struggling to figure out what exactly she did that had exceeded all expectations. Likewise, she must have wondered what type of behaviours that her teammates liked about her.
- **Adopt the appropriate behaviour of active engagement in a positive manner:** The manager in the above example oversimplified his messages to the point that it did not help the receiver of the feedback on anything. The manager did not make any future suggestions or recommendations either.

We have covered a lot about giving feedback to your direct report and the process that takes us there but there is another scenario where feedback should also be given upwards, namely to your manager or the management team or someone higher up the chain of command. This can be daunting and in fact scary as there is a lot more at stake here than just giving feedback but potentially your career.

Giving Feedback Upwards

In most situations, people back away from giving feedback and take the attitude of 'it is just not worth it' justification. I have chosen at times not to give certain feedback to my manager or the management team for fear that it would not be well taken or that it in turn might jeopardize my relationship with my direct manager. However, I have also on many occasions given feedback to my manager and his manager because I trust they are open and will take all feedback and evaluate them appropriately as the culture of the organisation is one that is self-critical, open and honest for discussions and disagreements.

The only question about giving feedback to your manager is whether you **trust** him or her enough to know that feedback will be taken appropriately. I have also observed that the managers who are most open to receiving feedback are those who are secured in their positions and whose desires are for the continuous improvement of themselves, the team and the company.

Now that we have established that we can give feedback to our managers, the question becomes, would the style of feedback be different? After much trial and error, I think that the basic four elements are the same and should be used regardless of the status or position of the person as the feedback addresses issues and provides point of clarification and recommendation about the issue and not about the person. Once again, the objective of the feedback should be to improve an issue and not as a judgment or criticism of the person.

I have learned over the years that to give feedback to my manager or upwards, requires a different approach as the consequences could be significant:

- **Trust and Openness of my manager**. Is my manager open to feedback? Do I trust my manager enough to give feedback without any negative consequences? I have worked with some great managers who are smart, experienced and confident enough to be open to feedback, and that is great because the quality of the discussion is enriching and encouraging.
- **Severity of the issue**. Is the issue or problem severe enough to be brought up? Can it be solved at my level? If it can be handled, then be part of the solution and work it out and settle the issue. If it cannot be, then decide to bring it up.
- **Be prepared** and ensure that it is specific, significant, well understood and suggestions are in place to be discussed.

Once again, it is important that in any organisation, we are able to give feedback to managers and upwards and each of us owe it to ourselves to learn and grow continuously. Pick your feedback and gauge for yourself when feedback needs to be given to your manager. Like all actions there are reactions to be expected. With any feedback, the motivation can lead to something positive or negative and the difference in the two is whether it will help you be better and improve your performance. Sometimes you don't have a choice but to give feedback as the consequences of not giving feedback is more damaging to you or your team.

People strive to be better, to compete harder, to be the best because ultimately the feedback that you desire to have is in these simple words . . . Well DONE! So why should I care about feedback? It's because I want to be better than where I am today.

Key Ideas for Giving Feedback

- Be clear on the **purpose** of the feedback: **Reinforce or Rectify**

- **4S** elements of relevant feedback are:
  - o Specific
  - o Significance
  - o Seek to understand
  - o Suggestion

- 'Fit-to-Purpose' Approach
  - o Timing and Frequency
  - o Appropriate Environment
  - o Communication method

- Preparation on How to Conduct the Feedback Session
  - o Ensure that the information presented is valid.
  - o Adopt the appropriate behaviour of active engagement in a positive manner.

---

4 Receiving Feedback

"He who frowns when they say he sucks shouldn't smile when they say that he rocks."
—Mokokoma Mokhonoana

Equally important in feedback is how to receive feedback. This is because the next step to improvement lies in our abilities to receive feedback. Therefore, it is critical that we also learn the key elements in how to receive feedback effectively in order to get the most out of feedback.

> **Be open to receive feedback** in the same manner as you are open to giving feedback.

Key Elements To Receiving Feedback

There are a few key elements that are important to remember and the ones that I have learned over the years to apply:

- **Purpose and Intent of feedback**. It is for positive and continuous improvement and learning. The heart must be

54

prepared before the mind to be able to hear and process. I believe that the giver of the feedback has the best intentions when giving me the feedback.

- **Be open to the feedback.** Each of us has blind spots. There are areas that we are not able to see about ourselves but clear to others around us.

- **Take key takeaways from the feedback.** There will always be something to learn so take the positives and have an open attitude to identify it.

- **Decide on whether an action plan is required.** You are free to decide on what you want to do with the feedback and whether anything is required after that. If the feedback is important to you, work out an action plan to put it in place.

- **Check back.** To go back to the giver of the feedback and check again to see if any improvement(s) was noticed assuming that you did put in place an action plan and decided to act on it. This is a step that is usually missed out. But it is a good step to remember just to check ourselves to see if it has been observed and whether its outcome was achieved.

From my personal experience, there have been some great feedbacks which were tough but fair and left me feeling disappointed, and yet were clear on what I needed to do to improve. Strange as it may be, it is these tough but fair feedbacks that I valued the most as they were clear on specific areas that needed to be worked on.

How To Receive Feedback

When receiving feedback:

- **Encourage feedback and listen well:** Be proactive and seek for feedback in your pursuit to improve yourself. React positively to feedback. Any information that you can obtain about yourself from others would help you to know others' perceptions and if valid, areas for improvement. Proactively ask questions such as the following:

o How did I come across just then?

o Did you notice what I did poorly in the recent product launch?

o Are there any specific areas of improvement that you want to share with me as far as handling difficult customers are concerned?

- **Seek clarity of what is being said, do not be defensive:** Be calm when receiving feedback. Do not jump to any conclusion or start being defensive as this may discourage the person giving the feedback to continue to share their observations. As a matter of fact, it is critical for you to clearly understand their feedback. You have to ask them very specific questions to understand the behaviours that you need to change. For example, if someone says that "you did awful in your recent product launch", your response would be to ask for specific or more information:

o What did I do that demonstrated I was awful in my recent product launch? Which specific area did not meet your expectations?

The main purpose is to derive the description of a specific behaviour from the person giving the feedback rather than trying to justify your action.

- **Ask clarifying and qualifying questions:** Two types of questions that are very effective when receiving feedback are clarification and qualification questions. Here are the examples:

o **Clarification questions:**

- What did I do that made you think I was rude to the customer?
- Why are you not happy with my performance?
- In what area did I fail to meet your expectation?

o **Qualification questions:**

- I heard that you mentioned I was not interested in the new role. May I understand your assumptions in saying that?
- You were not happy with my way of handling the client's objection. Were you not happy about the intonation of my voice or the explanation that I provided?
- In the past month, did you observe specific situation that I engaged in such behaviour?

- **Validate the feedback with others:** Try to get a balanced view from others as well. You would want to know whether or not others (who are relevant) think the same way or have the same perceptions about you. That may not necessarily be the case. By doing this, you would have a much balanced view on where you stand. This would guide you in deciding the best course of action to take moving forward.

- **Summarise understanding and agree on specific actions:** Once you have received all the feedback, make a point to summarise your understanding of the feedback. Agree on specific actions that you would want to execute to improve your behaviours. Thank the person who gives the feedback.

- **Do something about it:** The most important thing is to take action. It is worth your while to take time and reflect on the feedback. Internalise the key learning and execute the agreed action items. Make a point to assess your progress over time and recognize your improvement accordingly.

All feedback has the positive intent of helping you to improve and grow. As a manager, receiving feedback can be difficult as we can be caught up with the notion that 'we know it all' or 'have experienced it all' and therefore it is even more important for managers to set aside his or her pride and be open to learning and improving.

How we handle receiving feedback will also determine whether people will continue to give feedback or not. If your reaction towards receiving feedback is negative, angry, defensive and so on, you can be assured that you will be receiving very little useful and honest feedback in the future. Feedback as mentioned above is NOT a one way street and therefore in order for it to be a productive two way street, you must be able to receive feedback with the same level of maturity and openness you would expect of someone you are giving feedback to.

When Do We Ask For Feedback?

When and how we ask for feedback from our peers, direct reports and managers need to be decided. For me, it is a regular monthly rhythm that I would have with my peers, direct reports and manager where it is a face to face and one on one meeting. The discussion would focus on work/business updates and then feedback on me as well as my feedback for them. I think that it has served me well and with frequent update session, there should not be any surprises at the end of the year during performance review.

Suggestions for regular feedback session:

- **Monthly meeting**. Set it in the calendar as recurring monthly and keep to it. This sets a certain consistency and in a very busy environment you will at least be able to have quality discussion with your direct reports as well as manager in an environment that is scheduled and prepared for.

- **Weekly 'transactional' meetings.** Weekly meetings are typically operational or transactional in nature. Therefore focus on the objectives of the meeting and note down any behavioural feedback for the monthly meetings or in a separate discussion.

Of course all this can only take place if both parties are open and honest with their respective feedback and not just try to maintain the 'peace'. I have personally been in a number of situations, where confronting someone with negative feedback would have been very challenging, knowing how the person will react to anything negative and therefore the question becomes, is it better to keep the peace or to be courageous enough to give the feedback?

I have also learned that the subsequent question that I should ask is *"what is the outcome of the feedback?"* and *"is it significant or impactful?"* There are times when the person will not accept the feedback and will retaliate instead; then keeping the peace is the most appropriate course of action in the short term. However, in the longer term, I would doubt it.

I have also learned that asking for feedback is very dependent on the culture of the organisation that you are in. There are some work environments where the culture is to maintain the status quo and feedback is not welcomed or expected. This could well be the culture that you are in and I would challenge you to be the agent of change. Start by asking for feedback, not giving feedback. You might be surprise with areas that can be improved on. Once people experience how you receive feedback openly, it will open up further discussions.

There are of course situations and times when feedback is given to you without you asking or seeking for it. Such feedback though not on your terms, is equally important. As it is not on your terms, the feeling of loss of 'control' will play a part in how you will respond and it is therefore always critical to practice listening and understanding before reacting. This is of course easier said than done but with practice it can be mastered.

There are usually 2 main reasons why someone would proactively give you feedback:

- They are very upset with you and just need to let you know about it.
- They care about you and want to help you out proactively.

Regardless of the reasons, how you listen and handle the feedback is more telling than how the improvements or changes are made. The hardest thing not to do is to be upset, angry or retaliate; hence the best advice would be to listen, understand and keep *quiet* as an emotionally charged situation is never made better by being emotional too. There is no need to give an immediate response as feedback is not a task to be completed, it's a process to be reflected upon for improvements.

> **Feedback does not require immediate response.**
> **It should be reflected upon.**

Therefore a simple process to follow would be to (1) Thoughtfully Reflect, then (2) Honestly Assess and (3) Commit to Improve as depicted in the example below:

Your manager walks to you and says "Let's talk, I have some feedback for you." Both of you walk to his room and sit down as naturally and casually as possible. Running through your mind all this while is 'what happened?', 'what wrong have I committed?', 'who is this person who brought this out?' and of course 'it's not my fault!' He begins by saying that he received some feedback from 'some' people about the team and that they are not performing up to expectations and not delivering on their deliverables as per the agreed deadline. He then proceeds to ask you to explain.

So how would that look like?

What are you going to do?

Possible response:

A. Be defensive. Your response could be something like this. "Who said that?", "Which deliverable?", "It's not true!"

B. Seek to understand and obtain more information. You could say "I would like to know more information so that I can understand the situation better and give a better account of what this is about."

C. Be the victim. You could respond by giving out a whole list of excuses as to why it's so difficult to deliver or just how inappropriately resourced you are.

In this situation, if we follow the 3 steps above of Reflect, Assess and Improve, it would look something like response B. You would ask for more information and clarification from your manager and it could go something like this, as depicted below:

I would like to have **more information and specific details** *if possible as I would like to ensure that everything is on track and that other teams are supported and receiving what was committed to them. Therefore in order for me and my team to do that, I need to have some specific details.*

The manager then explains in more detail the feedback and possible ways of overcoming the issue. You then take in all the information, reflect upon each area without feeling defensive of you or the team and honestly assess the situation and commit to making the necessary adjustments.

In Chapter Three, we talked about feedback being specific. In this scenario we will need to ask for specifics as well. It is through specific feedback that we are able to make improvements. The danger of a general or generic feedback is that it does not provide any valuable information for an improvement plan. It also leaves a lot to interpretations and speculations which are not useful.

It is critical to remember that work is about issues and problems that need solving and not a personal attack on you as a person. When you are able to distinguish between the two, it is much easier to receive feedback. It is never easy to separate you as person with the work that you do but I have learned over time that unless that happens, you will take everything personally. That will stop you from growing as you would either deny or defend your position. That will lead to no improvements. The fear of negative feedback should not be understated. Franklin D. Roosevelt said "Only Thing We have to Fear is Fear Itself."

What To Do With The Feedback

It is great that now we know how to give and receive feedback, the next and probably most important aspect of feedback is this: **What do we do with the feedback?** It is fair to expect, that we should take the feedback and change for the better. However, as we all know, change is harder than just saying that we will change. Change requires that we make modifications in our habits, behaviour, work styles, communication styles and so on. To make change possible, there are a few aspects to consider:

- **Level of Commitment**. How high is our level of commitment to make that change?
- **Necessity of the Change**. Is the change worthy or necessary?
- **Difficulty of the Change.** How difficult is it to make that change?

Let us look at the example below:

If the feedback is related to improving your health by lowering your blood pressure, stress and cholesterol levels, needing you to exercise at least 30mins a day three times a week. How would you assess this based on the 3 criteria above on a scale of 1 to 10?

Commitment

1	2	3	4	5	6	7	8	9	10

Necessity

1	2	3	4	5	6	7	8	9	10

Difficulty

1	2	3	4	5	6	7	8	9	10

If I were to take this, I would rate my level of commitment at 8, necessity as 9 due to my health concerns but difficulty at 9. This would determine that I know that it's going to be difficult but because I know that it is necessary and I am committed to it, my chances of making this change is high, at least for a short period of time. I also know that if I were to put this into action for at least 30 days, I might be able to develop a new habit and routine that would include exercise in my weekly schedule. On the reverse, if my commitment level is low and the difficulty is high even though the necessity rating is high, I will most probably not be very successful in making the change.

Therefore we need to be very honest with ourselves as to whether change is possible. There are however many alternatives to make change possible. It can be done by breaking down the change to smaller, more manageable and less difficult components.

> **Break down changes to smaller, more manageable components**

Following the same example above about exercise, if I am to take a 5 min walk every hour around the office or walk up one flight of stairs or park slightly further, then the level of difficulty may not be as high as was first thought. Then, coupled with the high level of commitment and high level of necessity with relatively lower difficulty, change is much more possible now.

Let's take a very common example in the workplace.

You were given feedback that you are always late for meetings, affecting the meeting flow and showing disrespect to the people attending the meeting. What are you going to do about that?

Commitment									
1	2	3	4	5	6	7	8	9	10

Necessity									
1	2	3	4	5	6	7	8	9	10

Difficulty									
1	2	3	4	5	6	7	8	9	10

You will need to decide where this feedback is placed on the scale. Just remember if you don't believe that it is necessary, commitment will not be high even though the level of difficulty could be low and therefore no change will take place. We need motivation to drive our commitment level and necessity is the key to driving motivation. I know that it is a simple feedback and I used to struggle with it too as my calendar could be jam packed with back to back meetings. After a little while, I realized that I was in far too many unnecessary meetings or that the meetings were not conducted effectively. Hence they would run late which will in turn affect the next meeting. Therefore the change that needed to take place was either not to attend certain meetings or when I did attend, have a very clear set of agenda and items to go through and stay focused on them.

Key Ideas For Receiving Feedback

EAR

- **Engage** in the discussion by actively listening to what is being shared and be open and not defensive.
- **Ask** clarifying and qualifying questions and gather more information so that you are able to understand the intent and the desired change.
- **Review** the action plan if necessary.

SECTION 3:

Different Types of Feedback

5 Internal Feedback

"I think it's very important to have a feedback loop, where you're constantly thinking about what you've done and how you could be doing it better."
—*Elon Musk*

The internal based feedback would centre around what happens or takes place within the confines of the workplace as well as any company wide survey or feedback mechanism that exist.

These typically range from one on one session based on observations to more holistic approach which incorporates feedbacks from managers, peers and direct reports. In this particular chapter I would like to only highlight 3 types of feedbacks:

- Observation based feedback.
- 360 degree feedback.
- Internal Company wide survey/feedback.

Observation based Feedback

The most common basis for feedback is based on observation. We tend to perceive and evaluate everyone and everything whether we realised it or not. If someone says something out of line or makes a brilliant remark, a certain perception of that person is formed.

Let us see what this would involve:

John has a direct report Adam, who was very smart, tough negotiator, thoughtful and was delivering on his commitments. However, the feedback that John received about Adam from his peers was different from John's perception of Adam. Adam was having issues working with other team members and in fact was even accused of bypassing certain processes to achieve his goals.

Therefore what John observed did not form the full picture of Adam as it was only based on one side of the equation. Observation based feedback must be validated with data gathered from multiple sources else it will be an incomplete assessment of an employee.

What are some of the things to look out for from observational feedback?

- It is based on what you observe and experience with the person. It is one dimensional in nature.
- Diversity in the work place will mean that each of us will be dealing with people from different background, experience and culture. It is important that we do not judge others based on our set of values.

My advice is to try and not judge and formulate a certain perception of any individual. Be gracious. I know that it is hard in most situations but I truly believe that it will serve you well in the future when you are able to separate work related expectations vs. whether the person is good or bad.

Let us take an example where this can play a part.

Jack is a hard worker and is always committed on executing what he has committed to. He will push and drive members in the team to achieve it. To his manager, Jack is great as he gets results and makes things happen but to his peers, they see him as arrogant, insensitive and unreasonable. There is probably truth on both sides as John perceives himself as someone who will get the job done regardless of the obstacles and will relentlessly drive the team to get there. As a manager, what would you do when you hear the negative feedback about John not being a good team player or a team lead?

Possible responses:

A. You would defend John and say that the results are being delivered and that's all that matters.

B. You would defend John and then figure out what is the best way to give feedback to John on how he can think about making changes in his interaction with his peers for future projects.

C. You would tell the people who are complaining to tough it out.

D. Just listen and don't do anything about it.

I have tried all the above at some point in my career and I am not going to say that I have achieved 100% success but it has provided me with my own sense of experience and perception as to how best to handle the situation and the person.

I have come to learn that feedback starts with listening. Listening to what you see, listening with your ears when they communicate with you and those around them and listening to what your heart tells you. Let me elaborate further on this.

Observational feedback is really about how we gather information that is around us and to do that we must listen to what message is being communicated. We do that through our eyes which see and observe how someone interacts and relates with others. We conclude its appropriateness and effectiveness to the requirements of the role. We listen with our ears to hear what is being communicated, the depth of the discussion and content as well as the subject matter. Finally we listen with our hearts, to understand the motives and thought processes.

> **Feedback starts with observing and listening**

It is with all these information that we make a range of opinions and compile feedback that is relevant on the employee. Most important of all is what our heart is saying about the **purpose** of the feedback. If feedback is made with the best intention, for the continuous improvement of the employee, then do not hesitate. Go do it. But if there is any doubt or misplaced intention, think through it, and decide if the feedback should still be given, as an employee can see right through it.

360 Degree Feedback

As the name suggests, a 360 degree feedback is a method by which employees receive confidential and anonymous feedback from people who work around them. This would include manager, peers and direct reports and your own self-assessment. This is to ensure that there is a 360 degree view of you as each of us will interact and react differently depending on whom we deal with. If you are consistent in your approach, each of these groups would essentially give rather similar feedback.

This feedback is typically gathered through a specific set of questions which will cover competencies that is expected of an employee or manager and each question will have a rating system in place. Along that rating scale, each person will have to rate or rank the person that the feedback is for. The person receiving the feedback will also fill out the same survey that others receive.

The reason organisations conduct this type of survey is to get a better understanding of their strengths and weaknesses based on competencies that are valued in the organisation. Based on what is identified, a development plan can then be put in place. Therefore this type of survey:

- <u>Measures behaviours and competencies,</u> feedback on how <u>others perceive</u> you.
- <u>Addresses soft skills </u> such as how well you listen, plan and set clear goals.
- <u>Acts as a framework to assess subjective areas</u> such as effectiveness, teamwork, leadership and character.

The 360 degree feedback [10]is not meant to:

- Assess you against your performance objectives.
- Assess your technical skills required to perform a role.
- Evaluate whether you are meeting the basic job requirements.

My personal experience below describes how the 360 degree feedback program is an effective tool in developing my skills around specific competencies.

I remember the first time I heard about the 360 degree feedback program, I was both excited and nervous. Excited as I was very interested to know more about myself and what others perceived of me and nervous because I did not

---

[10] Customer Insight, "What is 360 degree feedback?" http://www.custominsight. com/360-degree-feedback/what-is-360-degree-feedback.asp

want to know about my weaknesses. We had a session by the company that was conducting the program and were reminded that the feedback is meant to help in developing skills around key competencies that are required to be an effective manager in the organisation. The goal is to know where my strengths and weaknesses are and upon which development plans can be put in place.

Now I was surprised when I saw my report as my own perception of 'me' in some areas were so different from what others perceived. As an example, I was surprised with Empowerment as a competency. I have always perceived myself as being empowering but it turned out that my direct reports thought that I was not very empowering. And to top it off, my manager thought that I was too empowering and that my direct reports needed a little more 'guidance'. Now, what do you do when you have results like that?

To bridge the perception gap sometimes it requires minor behavioural adjustments such as how I was to assign a project or ask whether an employee needed more information.

The most important thing to recognise is that I needed to be open and honest with myself and needed the desire to work through areas that were challenging to me. These results are helpful but only as useful as you want it to be.

I believe that there are a few key areas that we need to be mindful of:

- **No tool or survey is perfect so don't over analyse them or give excuses.** I have come to learn that it's best to understand the intent of each feedback tool and method and take the best out of it.
- **Check your ego and keep it out.** The first thing that is affected by any feedback whether it's a structured feedback program or not, is the ego. Each of us has it and whether we dare or want to admit it, it does play a big part in how we conduct ourselves.
- **Perception is never one sided** and it is never complete or all encompassing. We each see what we want to see and only from

areas that we can see. Hence this type of survey can give you insights to what you might not be aware of.

- **Be honest with yourself.** Even if you are not, others will be. Some areas are harder to acknowledge but it is worthwhile to reflect and as the saying goes, "No Pain No Gain".

- **It is OK to not know everything** as your direct reports know it. Being a manager is a journey of learning and the best managers are those who acknowledge what they don't know and ask for help and even build a team of people who have skills and knowledge that complements the gaps. So managers are not Mr or Miss Know-It-All.

- **You are NOT going to be great in every competency that is required.** Perfection is not required and it is not like a test where you need to score 100%. It is a scale and ranking based on your strengths and weaknesses, and what others perceive it to be. I find that the most important aspect is what you know to be your strengths and weaknesses are consistently acknowledged by those around you. This is based on how you demonstrate them.

- **Making the change.** Each of us need to be committed to making the change else feedback does not have any benefits. So be committed and persistent in the pursuit for improvements.

Internal Company Wide Survey/Feedback

There are some organisations that conduct a yearly 'satisfaction' survey for their employees to get a pulse in terms of how their employees are feeling and thinking about certain areas such as the following:

- Work life balance.
- Meeting the needs of the employees.
- Relationship with customers and partners.
- Function of teamwork and cross group collaboration.
- Performance of their direct managers.

The end goal of these types of survey is to establish how the company as well as the employees are doing in the face of 'internal' expectations and perceptions.

As an example, in a company I worked for, a yearly survey was conducted to find out the internal pulse of the organisation around a few key categories such as how the management team is setting vision and empowering its employees, how it responds to customer and partner's feedbacks, how each employee sees his or her work life balance and so on.

As managers in the organisation, each are encouraged to understand how their teams are responding and 'feeling' about each of those categories and to put in place action plans to ensure that issues are addressed as a team. This is one survey where everyone has a role to play and not just the manager as the survey is based on each employee's feedback. This is a great tool for the employees, managers and the organisation as it enables every level of the organisation to participate in changes that are relevant to each other.

As with all feedback tools there are positives and negatives as to how it is perceived and utilised.

Here are some of the positives:

- Companywide survey where each employee, whether Chief Executive Officer or the Secretary, has a say. Everyone is able to give feedback to the company on areas where one believes are good and on areas where one would like to see changes take place for the good of the company. Therefore everyone is encouraged to participate in the survey.
- Gives a good overall perspective of how a group or department or unit is thinking and feeling about specific topics or areas of concerns as well as to highlight areas that are going on well. The ability to drill down on the results from companywide to groups makes it a great tool for each member of the group to then participate in improvement plans on categories that require it. *As an example, the No.1 companywide concern is Work/Life Balance but in Team A, the No. 1 concern is Customer and Partner*

Satisfaction and in Team B, the No. 1 concern is Job Satisfaction and so on. Therefore having the ability to drill down to each team or group makes the results relevant to the group. Specific actions can then be taken to solve a unique situation pertaining to the relevant group. Improvement plans that are relevant for the department or group can be developed and this is probably the most useful aspect of the survey. As the issues are particular to a department or across the organisation, the solutions to making improvements can be very "personalised" to each department as the people who make up that group are different in terms of roles and what is importa*nt for them. As an example, Team A and Team B both have issues with Work/Life Balance. Team A's improvement plan is 'Schedule last meeting by 4pm'. Team B's improvement plan is 'Working from home option'.* As you can see the issue is the same but how each team goes about dealing with the issue can be different so long as it addresses the concerns of the team members and everyone is committed to following it.

Some of the negatives:

- Participating in the survey without having the right perspective and using it as a tool or medium to provide negative feedback anonymously. It is critical that the feedback is honest and objective.
- Taking the results personally. It is difficult for a manager not to take the results personally especially if it is negative. Having experienced this myself, I have also learned along the way that if I am honest with myself, the results should not be a surprise if over the course of interacting with your team, you are listening to their feedback. How you take the results and turn them into positives is what is required as a manager.

How Should You Use Feedback?

I believe that this is one of the best tools to use to bring your team together and to get each member of your team to be accountable for his or her job satisfaction.

The action plan should be a consensus of how each team member will behave and respect another's work styles and priorities. Fostering team cohesiveness and understanding how each member works are extremely important for a leader as this will ensure how hard tasks are tackled and how group or team success is achieved and celebrated.

Key Idea For Different Types of Feedback

Think of "YOU"

- **Y**our view through **observation**

- **O**thers view of you through **360 degree feedback**

- **U**ber view of you from a **Company-wide survey**

6 External Feedback

"One of the things I've learned is to be receptive of feedback."

—Ben Silbermann

External feedback in this context refers to the information derived from some form of surveys conducted with your external stakeholders such as customers or business partners.

The key focus for this chapter is to provide guidance on what to do with the information gathered or the survey results that you have derived.

Whenever you receive data or information from an external survey, you have to follow up with the External Feedback Analysis Process as depicted on the next page, to be able to come up with the right course of action.

External Feedback Analysis Process

External Feedback Analysis Process

The processes involved are:

- **Know**: Know your current position. You need to have a baseline in order to analyse and assess new data or information to make any sense out of it. In addition, knowing your baseline would also help you to map out the right course of actions upon complete analysis and deductions of the data you acquired.
- **Capture**: Capture all the data from the survey conducted.
- **Analyse:** Based on the data captured, conduct a proper analysis to understand specific situations. Establish relevant hypotheses and scenarios as relevant.
- **Conclude:** Conclude your analysis with specific recommendation to move forward.
- **Act:** Implement the specific recommendation.

An example on how to apply these processes is depicted in the scenario below:

Oscar has just received the results of the 2013 Customer Satisfaction Survey last week from the third party contractor that his organisation hired to conduct the survey. He went through the report. He further summarised his department's position as presented below:

- The 2013 Customer Satisfaction result for his department was 88%.
- One issue that his customers were not satisfied about is their inability to complete the projects on time.
- During the year 2013, key improvements that the customers recognized were good response time as committed in their Service Level Agreement with the customers and impressive product knowledge among his sales team.

Based on the above findings, Oscar begins to analyse further in order to establish the future course of action. Using the External Feedback Analysis Process, he performs the following:

1. **Know**: He knew that his Customer Satisfaction result in the previous year of 2012 was 85%. The top three issues that had impacted the department's customer satisfaction results were:

   1. *Failure of Oscar's team to meet the 2 hour response time stated in their Service Level Agreement (SLA) with their top tier customers.*
   2. *Lack of product knowledge among the sales team.*
   3. *Delay in the completion of key projects.*

In response to the 2012 results, Oscar launched the following initiatives:

- **2 hour response time:** (1) All sales and support personnel were assigned shared performance measures of 2 hour response time integrated into their performance plan. (2) A clear severity level escalations were introduced. For issues that cannot be solved within 2 hours, a standard communication template are provided for all sales and support staff to enable them to provide a consistent and clear communication to the customers on (i) current status (ii) what's being done (iii) what will happen next. (3) An issue case closure pack would be sent to customers when issues were resolved with a returned slip for customers to validate the closure of the case.
- **Lack of product knowledge among sales team:** (1)Sales team were required to attend all product sales training as well as pass the associated exams for each training class. (2) Brown bag product sharing session during lunch break twice a week.
- **Delay in completion of project:** (1) Improvement on the tendering and procurement process to expedite the award and delivery of materials. (2) Enforce 'scope freeze' for all the

requirements defined and signed off by the Project Steering Committee

2. **Capture:** The data captured by Oscar on the 2013 results demonstrated the following:

- Improvement of customer satisfaction score from 85% (in 2012) to 88% (in 2013).
- The improvement of 3 points was attributed to: (1)good customer service in meeting the 2 hour response time as documented in the Service Level Agreement. (2) Impressive product knowledge among his sales team.
- One area that remained an issue in 2013 was their ability to complete project on time. Evidently, the initiative launched the past year to overcome this issue did not bring the intended result.

3. **Analyse:** Oscar has to analyse why his 2012 initiatives to overcome delay in project completion did not bring about the intended results. Based on the data captured, the deduction was:

- **Improvement on the tendering and procurement process:** The improvement on the tendering and procurement process did bring significant result in meeting the project delivery on time. Issues on material delivery not meeting deadline was as low as 5%, a tremendous decrease from 50% in 2012
- **Enforcement of 'scope freeze' for all the requirements that were already signed off by the Project Steering Committee:** This initiative reduced the change request from 80% to 20%. While there was still some room for improvement its impact in timely delivery of project was minimal.
- **Substandard performance of subcontractors:** This was a new issue. The 2013 feedback from customers highlighted the specific scope and milestones that were behind time. 85% of those was

the scope performed by the subcontractors. This issue had impacted the timely delivery of projects immensely.

4. **Conclude:** Oscar came up with a conclusion that in the future, he needed to resolve the issue of substandard performance of his subcontractors. He conducted brainstorming session with his team members and the Project and consulting team. They finally agreed on these initiatives:

- Fortnightly project review checkpoint with their respective Project Managers.
- Penalty of 1% of project value for each day the project delayed.
- Mutually agree on alternative solution should skilled workers and/ or resourcing issues cropped up.

5. **Act**: Oscar and team had to follow up on the execution of the initiatives (Process 4) and measure its effectiveness in due time.

The Customer Satisfaction Survey 2014 would provide the data on how well the initiatives impact customer satisfaction.

The External Feedback Analysis process enables you to analyse the data captured by the survey in a structured manner and determine the best course of actions to further improve your situation or performance.

Key Ideas for External Feedback

- Focus on improvement.

- Decide on specific course of actions following the processes of Know, Capture, Analyse, Conclude and Act.

- Act!

SECTION 4:

Mastering Feedback Skills For Continuous Improvement

7 Power of Continuous Feedback

"I can't be a hypocrite as a coach because as a player that's what I wanted. I wanted feedback; I wanted communication from the boss. I showed up for work, you can yell at me if you want, but I want input. So that's the kind of coach I want to be."

—*Adam Oates*

World class organisations recognize the power of feedback for continuous improvement. They work hard on creating a feedback friendly environment. They encourage their employees to give and receive candid feedback. As a matter of fact, most of the organisations train their employees on how to give and receive feedback.

A sample case study, Scenario 7.1 is enclosed below to showcase how the organisation uses feedback for continuous improvement. Five key areas that will be discussed are:

- Business Review
- Performance Goal Setting
- Customer Service
- Project Monitoring
- Employee Engagement

Scenario 7.1

Innovative Solutions Limited (ISL)

Innovative Solutions Limited (ISL) is a 500 million application software company operating in China, India and the ASEAN markets (Singapore, Malaysia, Indonesia, Thailand, Philippines, Vietnam). Its flagship product is the iCRM, a Client Relationship Management solution targeted for enterprises, mid market as well as small businesses. The organisational chart of ISL is depicted below:

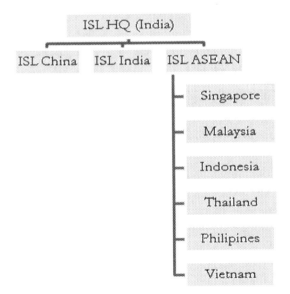

ISL ASEAN contributes 200 million or 40% of the total business for the ISL. Malaysia, one of the subsidiaries of ISL contributes 40 million or 20% of the ASEAN business. The Mid Market segment contributes 50%, the Enterprise Segment 37.5% and the Consulting Group 12.5%.

During the 2013 Financial Year, ISL Malaysia targets to grow by 12.5% which translates to revenue of 45 million. The Enterprise segment target is 17 million, the Mid Market segment 22 million and the Consulting Group 6 million. The organisational chart of ISL Malaysia is depicted below:

ISL Malaysia Organisational Chart:

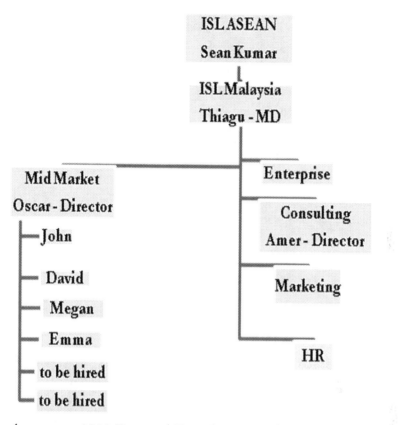

In the current 2013 Financial Year, there are a few key challenges that ISL Malaysia is facing which can potentially impact its ability to meet its targets as listed below:

- Consolidation of the telecommunications and banking industries has triggered heavy activities of mergers and acquisitions.
- Poaching of skilled resources within the industry create a challenged environment to retain skilled employees.
- High dependency on Mid Market segment to succeed with iCRM as the Enterprise segment is still behind other reputable CRM players such as Salesforce.com, SAP and Microsoft CRM.

Challenges for Oscar, Director of Mid Market Segment of ISL Malaysia:

Oscar has the following key priorities to be executed to ensure that he would be in the position to succeed in the 2013 financial year:

- Revisit his total opportunities and target. (Business Review, Scenario 7.1.1).
- Proactively negotiate his performance goals. (Performance Goal Setting, Scenario 7.1.2).
- Review his team's customer service performance. (Customer Service Improvement, Scenario 7.1.3).
- Review his top project status. (Project Monitoring, Scenario 7.1.4).
- Assess his employee engagement status (Employee Engagement, Scenario 7.1.5).

Business Review

ISL, like other major organisations have their own cycle of business planning and review. The typical business planning and reviews as depicted in Diagram 1[11] are:

- New Financial Year Kick Off, conducted at the beginning of each financial year.

  - o The New Financial Year Kick Off sets the tone for the new financial year. It comprises the yearly planned budget that

---

[11] Salwana Ali, A Handbook for First Time Managers: Critical Pointers That New Managers Need to Know to Succeed in Their Managerial Role (Singapore: Trafford Publishing, 2013), 41

details out the organisation's strategic initiatives for the year, its associated activities and resource planning and the commitment that every subsidiary, business divisions and product groups subscribe to.

- Monthly Business Updates, conducted at the end of every month.

  o The Monthly Business Update is a method to monitor the business progress of a unit, department, division or group. It is conducted via physical or virtual meeting.

- Quarterly Review, conducted at the end of every quarter of the financial year.

  o The Quarterly Business Review is a milestone check point to assess where a unit, department, division or group stands against the quarterly planned budget. Key focus is on execution and determining remedial or additional activities that needs to be done to position the business on track with planned budget.

- Mid Year Review, conducted in the middle of the financial year.

  o The Mid Year Review session is a half way checkpoint assessing the health of the business and what needs to be done to steer the business on course with the initial commitment to ensure that the annual target is met. Performance of every unit, department, division and group is reviewed. Key focus is also on execution, determining remedial and/or additional activities, resources and budget that need to be acquired to position the business on track with the planned budget and commitments.

- Financial Year Annual Review, conducted at the end of each financial year.

  o The Financial Year Annual Review session is the final check point of the organisation's overall performance consolidating the performance of each unit, department, division and group in the organisation. This session is also treated as the springboard to the following year planning session.

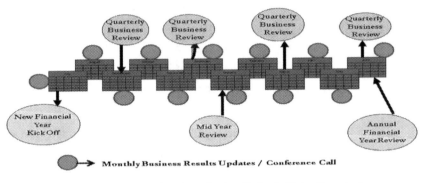

Diagram 1: Typical Business Review Cycles in Major Organizations

All the above business plan and review sessions have their distinctive formats and are highly structured with standard templates. However, in a nutshell the sessions are about getting to the bottom of:

- What exactly happened?
- What has worked?
- What has not worked?
- What would be done differently moving forward?

Scenario 7.1.1 demonstrates an example of a feedback engagement in a Mid Year Review session, between Oscar, Director Mid Market, ISL Malaysia and the ISL ASEAN Managing Director, Sean Kumar, together with his team members, Douglas Scott, Director of Retail Industry and Matt Baio, Director of Professional Services.

Scenario 7.1.1

The Mid-Market segment of ISL today has an installed base of 20 clients with a plan to add 3 new clients. Every new client is estimated to bring average revenue of 3 million. From Oscar's calculation, he would meet his 22 million targets by 3 new clients (9 million), product license upgrade from current installed base (10 million) and new license orders from existing clients that will complete the implementation of iCRM within the 2013 financial year (3 million).

However, the current consolidation of the telecommunications and banking industries coupled with fierce competition from the well-known multinational CRM solutions such as Salesforce.com, Microsoft Dynamics CRM and SAP have serious impact to Oscar's. His commitment of securing 3 new clients looks shaky due to the following reasons:

- Prospect 1, Excel Telecommunication is being bought over by another organisation.
- Prospect 2, Nippon Bank has a change of plan. It is now considering adopting the same solution as its Headquarters in Japan which happened to be SAP.
- Prospect 3, Happy Retail is still going on plan, though Oscar is anxious about its ability to decide on time.

Considering the current situation, Oscar has decided to request to call down on his commitment during the Mid-Year Review session. He has gone through his prospect pipeline to-date and at the current rate, the list does not look very encouraging.

Mid-Year Review Feedback Engagement:

Oscar presented his case to the Regional Senior Leadership Team of ISL, headed by the Sean Kumar, Managing Director of ISL Asean. As an overview, he presented the current state of the Mid-Market business, where it stood and the challenges it faced. Based on the overall situation presented, he then started to focus on his request to call down on his commitment as depicted below:

Oscar: Based on the current situation, I am considering calling down on my commitment . . .

Sean Kumar: What do you mean by calling down?

Oscar: I am confident of securing 1 new client, instead of 3.

Sean Kumar: You have a list of 30 qualified prospects in the system as far as your pipeline is concerned. And you have a track record of closing 1:8 the past years. I surely think that you are in the position to close 3 new clients based on the past track record, aren't you?

Oscar: I do have a list of 30 prospects in the system. However, based on my most recent review, only 50% of those prospects are qualified. In reality, I only have 15 qualified prospects at this point in time.

Sean Kumar: Hmmm . . . . are you telling me that the status of your prospects in the pipeline system is not up-to-date?

Oscar: Yes. I am afraid so. I am sorry for not being able to update it within time. However, here's the latest status of the qualified prospects, all 15 of them, which you can find in the presentation package Exhibit B.

Sean Kumar: <looking at Exhibit B> Ok. If you have 15 qualified prospects, why do you want to call down to 1 new client only?

Oscar: Because almost all of them are still in the evaluation mode of potential solutions. I expect them to take quite some time to go through the benchmark process, perform a proof-of-concept and so on. It will take some time before they are able to make decisions.

Sean Kumar: Let us recap what we have both understood so far. (1) There have been a few major changes in your accounts (2) Your Prospect 1, Excel Telecommunications has been bought over (3) Your Prospect 2, Nippon Bank has decided to follow its HQ direction in adopting SAP (4) Your Prospect 3, Happy Retail, you doubt that it would be able to decide within time (5) You have an additional 15 qualified prospects that you can work on for another 6 months, until the end of the financial year. Am I right in saying that?

Oscar: Yes, you are.

Sean Kumar: Do you seriously think that we have to call down? I mean, in reality, you do have 16 qualified prospects to work on. And going by your track record, you should be able to close 2 new accounts.

Oscar: <silent>.

Sean Kumar: Let's discuss on what we all need to do to help you close the account. Oscar, what do you need from us for your Prospect 3, Happy Retail to push them to decide on time?

Oscar: It would be good if we can bring Happy Retail to see a reference site within the same industry. We can potentially get our reference to cover on the implementation approach, potential pitfalls and how they have successfully secured the buy-ins from their users to use our CRM solution.

Sean Kumar: How would that guarantee that they decide on time?

Oscar: Currently, they like our solution which gives them the best ROI projection in comparison to other solutions. However, they are not sure of the most suitable implementation approach as they have lost a number of experienced IT resources recently. Another thing that they are not sure about is how best to secure buy-in from the CRM future users. I am confident that if we can get our reference to focus in depth on these two areas, they would be able to decide on our solution within the time that they initially planned.

Sean Kumar: Ok. We can do that. Douglas (looking at Douglas Scott, the Director of Retail Industry), please sync up with Oscar later and work on the reference site visit for him.

Oscar: Thank you. I will follow up with Douglas.

Sean Kumar: And Oscar, how about securing 2 more of your qualified prospects? What are you going to do about it?

Oscar: Among the 15 qualified prospects that I have now, I would focus most on these two accounts which are at the Proof-of-Concept stage. Proof-of-Concept would take around 60 days. Then, add another 15 days for the feedback submission from users. If the feedback is good, then they will move to the next stage of financial negotiations for the shortlisted 2 vendors, which may take between a month to three months depending on the complexity of the contract.

Sean Kumar: And what do you need from us to help you accelerate securing the 2 accounts?

Oscar: 2 technical resources that can help lead the Proof-of-Concept and develop the technical acceptance criteria as well. Our current internal expertise are lacking in that area.

Sean Kumar: Ok. <Looking at Matt Baio>, Matt, can you help source for the two technical resources for Oscar please?

Oscar: Thank you. I will follow up with Matt and provide all the required details soon.

Sean Kumar: Great. So, what do you think now Oscar? You would be getting all the help that you need to secure three new prospects. Should we maintain your commitment or should we low it down now?

Oscar: Considering all the help that is coming my way, I think the best is to maintain my commitment at securing 3 new clients.

Sean Kumar: Great. That's what I want to hear. And I believe you would be able to pull through with your commitment.

	Is there anything else that you would like to highlight within your space, Oscar?
Oscar:	No. I believe I have covered everything already.
Sean Kumar:	Fine. In closing, I would just like to summarise a few key points. Firstly, it is critical for you to ensure that your pipeline is current and up-to-date in the system at all time. We depend on those data and make a lot of key decisions based on them. Secondly, you must explore all possibilities to meet your commitment. Use everyone as a resource. Highlight the kind of help that you need to get closure clearly. I encourage you to take these observations on board.
Oscar:	Thank you for your feedback. I would seriously take that on board. Two things that I would be doing differently moving forward are ensuring that all my pipelines are current and up to date and exploring all possibilities to meet my target before even thinking of calling down. This session has certainly opened my eyes to appreciate the value of proactive dialogue and problem solving. Thank you so much.
Sean Kumar:	You are welcome. Good luck and win the business.

The feedback engagement between Oscar and Sean Kumar in Scenario 7.1.1 basically focuses on continuous improvement. Key observations that convey such message include the following:

- Sean's readiness to help Oscar to succeed in his tasks by asking all the **right questions** for Oscar to find the answers.
- Sean's approval in providing the kind of help that Oscar needs by getting his team to support and commit the appropriate resources to Oscar.
- Sean proactively highlighting the summary of learning from the review session and Oscar accepting such learning and agreeing on his future actions moving forward.

Performance Goal Setting

Performance management is a critical process in any business. However, the implementation of it varies. Most major organisations do typically have such process in place. The four stages of performance management are:

- **Plan:** Setting performance goal is the most critical activity within this stage. Other activities include induction, behaviours and competencies and planning personal development strategy.
- **Execute:** Employees carrying out the planned work with the manager's support.
- **Monitor**: Checking on progress made against the objectives and possibly new demands. Activities include 1:1 meetings, team meetings, customer feedback and peer review.
- **Review:** Acting on the information provided by the rest of the cycle so that an assessment of progress and achievements can be agreed on. Activities include actual performance review meeting as well as general planning on an on-going basis.

While organisations establish their strategic objectives and initiatives, employees are responsible and accountable to their own performances. Hence, they should take ownership of establishing the right performance goals for them during the year. For this reason, performance goal setting is an 'active' negotiation process between a manager and his or her subordinates.

An example of a feedback engagement to set performance goals (Plan stage) is depicted on Scenario 7.1.2.

Scenario 7.1.2

Oscar reports into Thiagu, the Managing Director of Innovative Solutions Limited. Recently, Thiagu hinted that he expects Oscar to grow his division by 5% this financial year. In Oscar's mind, that would mean maintaining high customer satisfaction of his existing installed base to secure new upgrades as well as securing at least 3 new clients. Oscar is sceptical about the 5% growth due to the current competition in the marketplace as well as his lack of sales resources. Currently, he has four direct reports with two more vacancies to be filled.

He has to negotiate with Thiagu to achieve a common ground on a realistic goal for him this year.

Performance Goal Setting Feedback Engagement

Oscar: I understand that we will be discussing on the performance goal setting today.

Thiagu: That's correct. It is your agenda. So, why not you start?

Oscar: Sure. I will be happy to do that. Let me start with the big picture first.

Thiagu: Ok. Sounds good to me.

Oscar: There are three things that I want to highlight. First, currently, two of our major industries, telecommunications and banking are going through the consolidation phase which has resulted in major changes. We expect a number of mergers and acquisitions happening in the next 24 months. The industry average growth for each sector is 3%. This represents a certain degree of risk for sure as far as customer acquisitions are concerned. Organisations would have the tendency to stall on critical decisions until they are clear of their directions. Secondly, the demand for skilled resources in sales and implementation of CRM is higher than supply. Many organisations are poaching resources from each other to get the best skilled and trained employees. Such situations have impacted our organisation as well.

A number of our own skilled resources have jumped ship to join either our customers or our competitors. We are struggling to hire the right sales people to join our team.

Thirdly, there seems to be over reliance on Mid Market segment to achieve our goals this year as the competitive situation in the Enterprise space is tough as the position of our iCRM solution in the Enterprise is still lacking behind in comparison to the likes of Salesforce.com, SAP and Microsoft CRM.

Thiagu: What do you think your performance goals should be for this year? What are your plans, Oscar?

Oscar: Based on the backdrop that I have talked about, I believe my goals should be the following:

1) Target growth of 3%, as equivalent to the industry growth.

2) Acquire 3 new customers in the Mid Market segment, worth 9 million.

3) Product upgrades on current installed base of 10 million.

4) New license orders from current implementation of 3 million.

5) Customer satisfaction of 80%.

6) Employee engagement score of 85%.

Thiagu: Why 3%? I think you can grow 5% this year just like the previous year?

Oscar: As I mentioned Thiagu, the current consolidation in the industry represents high risk of them stalling on their decisions.

Thiagu: Well, we do have strong installed base in these two industries though. Both in banking and telecommunications, 6 out of 10 customers are using our solution. When consolidation happens, there is also an opportunity for us to expand our solution further in the 'new' organisations.

Oscar: I doubt we can depend on that. Such situation would also give them the opportunity to review the whole environment which might trigger them to adopt something totally new.

Thiagu: Have you thoroughly considered other markets? Retail, Insurance and Manufacturing are another three major industries with high concentration of Mid-Market sized companies. Do we not have a strategy on how to win opportunities in these markets? In fact, maybe we ought to consider investing in these markets considering that the banking and telecommunications are challenging this year.

Oscar: I did think about that. However, I do not have enough headcounts to go around and prospect new opportunities. I just have enough resources to cover the current pipelines. I am still in the process of hiring the two additional headcounts. I cannot do a good job on prospecting other markets unless I manage to hire these two resources very soon.

Thiagu: Does that mean that you have not reflected all the opportunities in these three industries right now?

Oscar: No, I have not.

Thiagu: Why not?

Oscar: Since I do not have the sales resources to cover them, it is very hard for me to gauge the exact situations of our opportunities in these three markets. Hence, I decided not to include them to avoid having such a risky forecast being presented to you.

Thiagu: Ok. Sounds like you have good intention. However, I urge you to be open and transparent on the overall situation of your business by highlighting all the key factors, both, positive and negative.

Oscar: Ok. I will take note of that.

Thiagu: How can we explore to secure some business from these three industries? What do you think we should do?

Oscar: I need help to do aggressive recruitment for the two headcounts. Unless I can fill up these two heads, it is impossible for me to focus on the opportunities within the three industries.

Thiagu: Who has been helping you on the recruitment?

Oscar: Just the Recruitment Manager based on the applications that we received to date.

Thiagu: Ok. Let us consider getting internal referrals as well as get help from the Head Hunters. I will speak with the HR Director about it. We will treat your head counts as the priority.

Oscar: Ok. Appreciate your help.

Thiagu: With that, can you consider a growth of 5% now?

Oscar: Can we work on a stretch goal of some sort? I mean let's stick to 3% with a stretch to 5%. What do you think?

Thiagu: I can accept that for now. However, I would like to revisit that within the next 6 months. If you get the two positions filled, and we are on track by the 6th month milestone, I would like to review the goal again. We should be doing 5% growth. Is that acceptable to you?

Oscar: Sounds ok to me.

Thiagu: Great. Let's just summarise what we have discussed and learned so far. Firstly, we need to be open and transparent on all the situations; good and bad that are happening in our business. Secondly, always explore the best, push the envelope and if you think there are show stoppers or stumbling block, highlight that to me. Treat me as a resource. Then we can discuss and explore the solutions together. And finally, I still think we should be doing 5% growth. As agreed, you can treat that as a stretch goal for now while we hire the two headcounts to help you out. Within the next six months, we shall revisit the goals and review them.

Oscar: Yes, Thiagu. Appreciate your support and understanding. I will be open and transparent about the exact situations of the business, good or bad and will strive to put my best effort in everything I do. Also, I should be proactive in highlighting potential issues and reach out for help. And yes, I do agree that we should work on the stretch goal of 5% growth and review it within six months from now.

Thiagu: Great. Do you have any other questions?

Oscar:	Yes. What do you think of the rest of my goals?
Thiagu:	The rest are fine.
Oscar:	Great. I am all set then. Thank you.
Thiagu:	You are welcome.

The feedback engagement between Oscar and Thiagu in Scenario 7.1.2 basically focuses on continuous improvement. Key observations that convey such message include the following:

- Thiagu's effort to validate Oscar's plan of 3% growth by asking probing question to gain deeper understanding of his position.
- Thiagu's encouraging Oscar to stretch his goal with full support in putting aggressive plan to hire the new additional headcounts that Oscar needs for him to achieve such goal.
- Thiagu's emphasis on the value of open and transparent demonstrates his sincerity and readiness to take situations and challenges as they are (instead of just interested to hear the good news!) and proactively work on the solution with Oscar.

Likewise, Oscar benefited from the session immensely. He had great comfort in knowing that Thiagu was fully supportive of his plans. In addition, he felt even more motivated to do well due to the sheer commitment of Thiagu in prioritizing and committing resources to support him in his initiatives. Most important of all, Oscar knew that Thiagu trusted him to deliver as long as he had the right resources at his disposal.

Customer Service Improvements

Customer is the king. A good customer experience will enhance customer loyalty to organisations.

Major organisations strive to provide good customer experience.

Jet Blue for instance, delights its customers by providing the best customer experience. As Erika Andersen experienced in her Jet Blue flight from New York to Burbank, "the flight attendant was unfailingly kind and respectful to every passenger with whom she interacted during the six-hour flight. When she had to tell people to do something (for instance, getting me and the other passengers in the first row to put all our stuff up in the overheads), she did it with such an air of helpfulness ("I know this is a pain, but let's work together to make it happen") that no one minded at all. After we were underway, she handed me my computer bag and gave the woman next to me her purse, all without being asked and with a smile and a cheerful comment."[12]

Papa Hardware, a hardware company in Malaysia commits to delight its customers by compensating them with complementary products for any occurrences of late deliveries due to unforeseen circumstances. I ordered a Brush Cutter TL43 online on January 1st, 2014 and instantly, I received the order confirmation noting that the order was being processed. A day later, I received an email from Papa Hardware informing me that the Brush Cutter TL43 was out of stock and would only be available in a couple of months. As such, they upgraded my order to Brush Cutter TB43 (which cost a few hundreds more) at no additional cost and promised that the product would be delivered within three working days. When I did not receive the TB43 within the stipulated three days, I called Papa Hardware to check on it. The Customer Service Executive informed me that their logistics business partner was experiencing a number of service backlogs amid their relocating warehouses. He promised me that he would have the situation sorted out as soon as he could. He continued following up and updating me on almost a daily basis. I finally received my TB43 fourteen days later. Within that same week I received another package from Papa Hardware consisting of a complimentary product, the 7 pieces powerful

---

[12]   Erika Andersen, posted on Forbes.com, "I Love Jet Blue—Customer Service Done Right." Forbes.com, http://www.forbes.com/sites/erikaandersen/2012/03/19/i-love-jetblue-customer-service-done-right/

ratcheting screwdriver set together with a thank you note and a message of appreciation for giving them the opportunity to be of service. I was truly a happy customer despite the setback that I experienced as Papa Hardware responded well to my situation, upgrading my order at no additional cost, staying through until the end during the delivery hiccups and further compensated me with a complimentary product.

The most common measurement of customer experience is the customer satisfaction index. Annually, organisations conduct the customer satisfaction survey to find out how well they have served their customers in any given year. Based on the results of the customer satisfaction survey, they would decide on specific strategies and/or initiatives to be implemented to further improve the customer experience.

An example of a feedback engagement to establish customer service initiatives is depicted in Scenario 7.1.3:

Scenario 7.1.3

The customer satisfaction index for the Mid Market segment of ISL is currently 77%. Oscar reviews the result of the survey and notices that his department fell short due to the three month delay in two CRM implementations. The two clients have talked to a number of prospects about their experiences. Such situation has impacted ISL reputation to a certain degree in terms of its track record in delivering solution within budget and on time.

Oscar needs to find a fix. He has a customer satisfaction target of 80% this financial year, a 3 point increase. Oscar has decided to rally his team—John, David, Megan and Emma to brainstorm and decide on key initiatives to close the 3 point gap.

Customer Service Improvement Feedback Engagement

Oscar: Good morning every one. I appreciate your time attending this meeting. As per my email, our meeting objective today is to decide on the initiatives that we need to do this financial year in order to close the 3 point gap in our customer satisfaction score. Did you all go through the details of the customer satisfaction results that I emailed you recently?

All: Yes, we did.

Oscar: So, what do you think? Any views John?

John: I observed that there were two key reasons on why we were late in the implementation of our CRM solution in these two accounts. 1) Customer kept on changing their requirements and we entertained that (2) Availability of resources with the right skill sets.

David: Talking about resources, I agree on that. For my account, I have three different Project Managers during the 18 month project implementation. In fact, I felt embarrassed to go back to the customer every 6 months to introduce a new Project Manager. It gave the impression like they are not important.

Megan: Emma, why did you entertain them whenever they want to ask for new requirements?

Emma: It was so hard to say no.

David: There is no buy-in from the client. Hence, they always change their team composition during the requirement definition phase. We would end up repeating the whole definition process and the new people tend to ask for something different or totally new.

John: Did we not freeze the requirement definition at some stage? We do that in every project as far as I know. Why didn't we do it in these two accounts?

David: Obviously because we have changed too many resources in these two accounts. As I mentioned earlier, I had to introduce a new Project Manager every six months, within an 18 month project. I believe that really hurts the project.

Oscar: Ok. So we have two reasons that are related. (1) Moving target on requirement definition (2) Change of Project Managers too frequently. We can take a long term solution to resolve this. However, what do you think we should do to improve our customer service in these two accounts in the short term?

Megan: That's tricky. How about making sure that we deliver on time based on the latest schedule?

Emma: We definitely need to do that.

David: Even if we do that now, how would that help us in securing our 80% customer satisfaction target? They are already not happy with us.

Oscar: I think we do have enough time to fix it. Now we are in the first quarter of the financial year. The survey will be done in the fourth quarter. We have a few months to fix things and ensure that they recognize it.

John: Then, we need to prioritize and make sure that these two accounts get all the right resources in the project. And no one can leave until the project finishes, especially the Project Manager.

Oscar: Yes. I definitely need to plan constructively together with the Consulting team on the deployment of these resources. I will discuss with them in my next Project Monitoring Updates meeting a day after tomorrow.

Megan: We have to clearly spell out the new agreed schedule of completion, activities per milestone, deliverable per milestone and make sure we communicate progress to the right audience.

Emma: Also, I think at the high level, we should proactively get Thiagu, our Managing Director to meet up with the CEOs of the two accounts and update him on our progress.

Oscar: Sounds like we are getting somewhere. I heard from all of you that we should treat the two accounts as our key priorities until the implementations are completed. Our success factors are making sure that the projects are not moving targets and the key project resources, especially the Project Managers stay with the project till completion. We will schedule high level meeting between Thiagu and the CEOs of the two organisations to ensure that the CEOs are in the loop on the project status and what we are doing for them. We have to meet with the two clients and review the current project status. That will give us the opportunity to spell out the new agreed schedule of completion, activities per milestone, and deliverables per milestone as well as agreed on the right communication channel to communicate the progress of the project to the right audience.

John: Can we add one more thing Oscar?

Oscar: Sure. What is it?

John: I think one of us should attend the monthly Project Steering Committee meeting as well. To date, only the Consulting team attends.

Oscar: Do you all have time to do that? What about other commitments?

John: We are doing it only for just these two accounts. That's like an hour a month. Surely, we can allocate one hour for this important cause as it means a lot to our overall customer satisfaction score.

Oscar: What do you all think? Do you agree with John?

All: Yes. I agree.

Oscar: Great. I will also include that as our action item moving forward in addition to other points that I have summarised just now. Obviously, the Account Managers for these two accounts need to allocate that one hour a month to attend the Project Steering Committee meeting. Is there anything else?

All: No.

Oscar: Ok. That's it. Our meeting ends here. Thanks so much for your input.

The meeting held between Oscar and his team members, John, David, Megan and Emma in Scenario 7.1.3 basically focuses on how to improve the organisation's customer service in order to achieve their customer satisfaction target of 80%. Key observations that convey the emphasis of continuous improvement include the following:

- Oscar's assessment of the current Customer Satisfaction results and sharing it with his team members to get their views of the situation as they are in the field and are actively involved with the clients.
- Interactive discussions between Oscar and his team members demonstrate shared values on high performance and their commitment towards excellent customer service.
- Agreement on treating the two projects as key priorities, pushing Oscar to get the right resources who would stay with the project until completion, holistic approach to move forward and committing their own time to be involved in the monthly key meeting.

Project Monitoring

As far as projects are concerned, two key factors that would impact profitability in a significant manner are:

- Organisation's ability to complete project on time.
- Organisation's ability to complete project within budget.

As such, project monitoring is a very essential process for organisations to ensure that their projects are right on track, within a time frame and budget. During the project monitoring process, organisations would assess the following:

- Progress of project performance.
- Identify risks and constraints.
- Recommend plan adjustments.

An example of a feedback engagement to monitor project is depicted in Scenario 7.1.4.

Scenario 7.1.4

Following on his department meeting, Oscar has scheduled a meeting with the Director of Consulting, Amer, to discuss on the current project status of the two accounts that are currently behind schedule by three months. He would like to get to the bottom of the issues and propose the action plans that he has agreed with his team

Amer has agreed to meet with Oscar. He plans to provide the project updates for the two accounts that are currently behind schedule, based on the latest outcome of the project monitoring meeting that he had with his Project Managers.

Project Monitoring Updates Feedback Engagement

Oscar: Good morning Amer.

Amer: Good morning Oscar. So, I understand that you want to talk about the two accounts that are currently behind schedule.

Oscar: Yes. Absolutely, I need to discuss with you and see how best we can solve these issues and get the projects to complete as scheduled. We cannot afford to extend these projects further.

Amer:	Great. Let's talk about it. I have the latest status from the Project Monitoring meeting with my Project Managers yesterday. It is very timely.
Oscar:	I want to understand your views. How did we end up in such situations?
Amer:	Three reasons—(1) Too many changes in resources impact the project dynamic and stability (2) Poor communication and (3) Moving deadlines due to new requirements.
Oscar:	Can you please elaborate what poor communication means?
Amer:	We did a poor job at managing the communication between us and the customers. Oftentimes, our customers do not have the same understanding on our deliverables, the project status and issues.
Oscar:	Didn't we have Project Steering Committee (PSC) every month to update on project status?
Amer:	Yes. We did. We would end up repeating ourselves many times. Typically, these are issues or concerns that are being brought up by the users. The PSC members would share these during the PSC meeting.
Oscar:	What type of concerns did they have?
Amer:	Most are related to their acceptance of iCRM. Feedback such as it is not easy to use and there are just too much work that needs to be done to clean up their clients and prospect database. In fact, one department refused to use it totally.
Oscar:	That sounds like they are resisting change, are they not?
Amer:	Yes. They are.
Oscar:	Didn't we do change management for them?
Amer:	Yes and no. We trained 1/3 of the users so far. Then, we were not able to continue as planned schedule because our Change Manager left the company and it has taken us a while to get a replacement.
Oscar:	What was our fall back planning then?

Amer: Well, with such constraints that I have, I basically requested for a delayed schedule in the change management training which was approved in the PSC meeting.

Oscar: So, is the issue communication or the absence of a Change Manager?

Amer: The absence of a Change Manager is the compelling issue.

Oscar: Ok, which means we have two critical issues that need to be addressed—(1) change of resources too frequently or lack of resources with the right skill sets and (2) moving deadline due to new requirements. Are we in agreement on this?

Amer: Yes. And the two issues are related.

Oscar: Precisely. My team and I think that we should solve these issues together as we cannot afford to extend the time further. We would like for you to consider the following:

(1) We should treat the two accounts as our key priorities until the implementations are completed.

(2) Key project resources, especially the Project Managers should stay and other critical resources such as the Change Manager need to be filled in as soon as possible.

(3) Avoid moving target schedules. Let's freeze the requirement definition. We have to meet with the two clients and review the current project status. That will give us the opportunity to spell out the new agreed schedule of completion, activities per milestone, and deliverables per milestone as well as agreed on the right communication channel to communicate the progress of the project to the right audience. What do you think Amer?

Amer: How can you guarantee that our resources will stay? I am having such a hard time keeping them. Their skill sets are highly demanded now.

Oscar: How about bonus upon project completion? Not only for Project Managers, for the critical roles in the project as well such as Change Manager.

Amer: How are we going to convince our boss, Thiagu to do that?

Oscar: A few key reasons: Revenue, profitability, customer satisfaction, image and reputation. I think we have enough reasons to convince Thiagu to do it.

Amer: Do you really think we can make this happen?

Oscar: Yes. I think so. I am willing to give it a shot.

Amer: Great. Let me know what you need from me. I presume you would be building the business case to convince Thiagu to do that.

Oscar: Yes, I would. In the meantime, what do you think about our proposal to avoid the moving target schedules?

Amer: We have the same thing in mind. In fact, we have a meeting scheduled with the two clients to do just that.

Oscar: Good. On my part, I am also scheduling a monthly meeting for Thiagu to meet with the CEOs of the two organisations. We want to use that forum to update the CEOs on the project status, what we have done and highlight potential issues as well. We reckon the results ought to be consistent communication organisation wide.

Amer: Sounds good.

Oscar: Ok. Can we recap quickly on what we have agreed on? We agreed to proactively work together to place top priorities for these two accounts. Two issues that we need to solve effectively are to ensure that our resources stay all throughout the duration of the project and avoid the moving target schedules of the projects by freezing the current requirements. In addition, we will ensure consistent communications among project members and the various target audiences in the two organisations. My action items are to build a business case to convince Thiagu to award project completion bonus for all the critical resources in the projects. And Amer, your action item is to get agreement with the clients on the revised project schedule, deliverables per milestones, activities per milestones and renewed communication approaches to the respective target audiences, in your meeting with them next week.

Amer: That's correct. Thanks Oscar for your support.

Oscar: Sure. No problem.

The meeting held between Oscar and Amer in Scenario 7.1.4 basically focuses on assessment of current project status and brainstorming of potential ways to solve project issues. Key observations that convey the emphasis of continuous improvement include the following:

- Oscar's readiness and commitment to have a constructive discussion with Amer to find a resolution to the current project issues.
- Amer's openness to share the reasons of the project delays and strictly focusing on the core issues, rather than pointing fingers towards others for their failure to complete the projects on time.
- The seriousness to get the critical resources to stay on the project until project completion demonstrated by Oscar's willingness to build a business case to award project completion bonus to all the critical resources in the projects.

Employee Engagement

The definition of employee engagement according to Kevin Kruse, the author of the book Employee Engagement 2.0, is the emotional commitment the employee has to the organisation and its goals.

A highly engaged employee would put the extra effort to do whatever necessary for the benefits of the organisation. A procurement officer would stay for another thirty minutes after work to complete processing the invoices even when the boss is not around. A salesperson would spend time on Saturday to update the status of the sales cycle on the CRM system to make sure the information is relevant and current.

Organisations typically assess their employee engagement status on a yearly basis through the Employee Engagement Survey.

An example of a feedback engagement to improve employee engagement is depicted in Scenario 7.1.5.

Scenario 7.1.5

The result of the Employee Engagement Survey for Oscar's last financial year was 80%.

This year Oscar has to improve the score by 5 points, to 85%. He goes through the details trying to figure out what else he needs to do differently to get to 85%. He concludes two areas that he needs to improve on:

(1) Learning and development plan for his team members
(2) Clarity on career advancement opportunities

He decided to gather his team to seek their input on potential initiatives that he can implement in these two areas.

Feedback Engagement for Employee Engagement Improvement

Oscar: Good afternoon everyone. Thanks for making time to meet up today. My objective today is to seek feedback from all of you on your learning and development plan and career advancement opportunities. Three things that I want to find out are first, your views on the current learning and development plan, second, your views on career advancement opportunities and third, what do you want to see implemented this financial year within these two areas.

Emma: Wow! That's interesting. I appreciate your openness in seeking our views in such a transparent manner.

David: I feel the same way. And as far as I am concerned, I am having difficulty in assessing the kind of learning or

	skill sets training that I need to choose every year. What we have today is quite generic. I want something more tailored to my role.
Megan:	I agree with David. I think it would be great if we have a role based competency roadmap. Then, all I need to do is select from the list of learning and development plan required for my role and competency.
John:	In addition, I think it would be good also for us to discuss further on the unique development scope that we aspire during our 1:1 meeting with you. For example, I may want to explore being a project leader. We want the comfort feel that you are open to listening to our aspirations.
Oscar:	Wow! These are amazing feedback. How about career advancement opportunities? What are your views on this?
John:	I am not sure where to begin. I don't have a clue on what's the next step in my career is.
David:	Who should be planning our career plan? Do we plan it ourselves?
Megan:	Well, even if we were to plan it ourselves, we still need guidance from someone. Is it HR? Or is it you, Oscar?
Emma:	Yes. I am curious about that as well. It is hard to plan a career if we are not aware of what's available and not sure about our own readiness. I think career advancement goes hand-in-hand with our learning and development plan.
Oscar:	Well, it sounds like we have to start from scratch on this. I tend to agree with Emma that the career advancement goes hand-in-hand with your learning and development plan.
John:	As a starting point, why not we establish a role-based learning and development plan this year? I mean, whatever our role is, we should be able to access our learning and development roadmap and schedule a detail plan on the types of learning or training that we need to attend for the whole year.

Megan:	That sounds good. And I think at this juncture, we can take the career advancement discussion in our 1:1 session with you, Oscar. We can treat that like 1:1 career coaching session. I would imagine such discussion may happen once or twice a year. It is not really a monthly affair, is it?
David:	Yes. That makes sense. I see the whole initiative as a phased approach which we will keep on improving the system and process.
Emma:	I agree. Phased approach would be the best.
Oscar:	Great. I am just excited with all your enthusiasm and excellent feedback. All of you have recommended that we establish role-based learning and development plan to enable you to have a clear roadmap on the type of competency training that you need for the whole year. Since career advancement goes hand-in-hand with the learning and development plan, you have agreed that we treat this as a discussion that we will have during our 1:1 meeting session. We anticipate such discussion to happen either once or twice a year. We are taking a phased approach and will continue to improve the system and process as we go along. Did I capture everything that we have agreed?
All:	Yes. That sounds good.
Oscar:	Thank you so much. I appreciate your time and feedback. I will keep you all posted with the progress of this initiative during our future staff meetings as well as via emails.
All:	Ok. Look forward to that.

The meeting held between Oscar and his team members—John, David, Megan and Emma in Scenario 7.1.5 basically focuses on securing feedback from his team members on how to improve employee engagement. Key observations that convey the emphasis of continuous improvement include the following:

- Oscar's conviction and commitment to find out from his team members on their exact needs in learning and development and career advancement, the two areas which he was lacking in the Employee Engagement Survey done the previous year.
- The team members of Oscar being open and direct when giving feedback to ensure that Oscar is clear on their needs and aspirations.
- The team members of Oscar are serious and realistic about executing a good initiative demonstrated by their recommendation to go for a phased approach while pursuing improvement of system and process along the way.

The five business areas discussed in the case studies are some of the common areas where feedback is constantly required for organisations to improve their performance. In fact, companies that are responsive to feedback are typically winners in their respective industries. Some examples include Amazon, Google, Apple, Jet Blue, Coke and Starbucks.

The Power of Continuous Feedback

- Feedback is powerful.

- When acted upon, it drives continuous improvement in self and the group you belong to.

- Develop structured approach to feedback for your key business processes.

---

8 Honing Your Feedback Skills

"If we're growing, we're always going to be out of our comfort zone."

—John Maxwell

It is now time to practice your skills in giving and receiving feedback. Firstly, let us focus on practicing how to give feedback.

Giving Feedback

The critical steps in giving feedback are summarised below:

Steps to giving feedback:

- Gather Data
- Evaluate Data
- Give Feedback

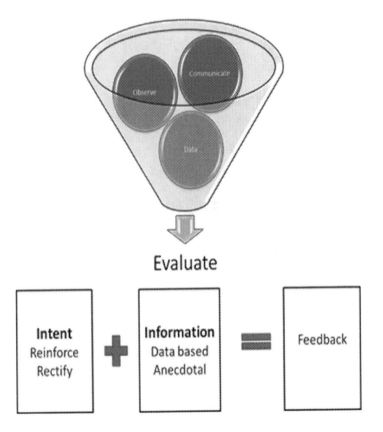

The above diagram depicts the critical steps in gathering and evaluating data, translating those data into meaningful information in preparing to give feedback that matters.

In addition, you have also learned that you will gain the value or benefits of feedback when the feedback given meets these criteria summarised on the next page:

Key Ideas for Giving Feedback

- Be clear on the **purpose** of the feedback: **Reinforce or Rectify**

- **4S** elements of relevant feedback are:
  - o Specific
  - o Significance
  - o Seek to understand
  - o Suggestion

- 'Fit-to-Purpose' Approach around timing, environment and communication method

- Preparation on How to Conduct the Feedback Session
  - Ensure that the information presented is valid.
  - Adopt the appropriate behaviour of active engagement in a positive manner.

You need to have a two prong approach to hone your skills in giving feedback:

- Follow the "3 Steps in Giving Feedback"
- Follow the "Key Ideas for Giving Feedback"

The two prong approach is presented below:

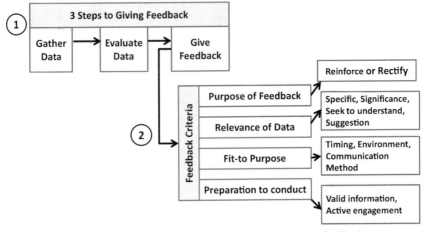

Two prong approach to hone your skills in giving feedback

Let us now focus on honing your skills in giving feedback by using the examples below.

Example 1: Honing your skills in a Business Review

Mid-Year Review Feedback Engagement:

Oscar presented his case to the Regional Senior Leadership Team of ISL, headed by the Sean Kumar, Managing Director of ISL Asean. As an overview, he presented the current state of the Mid Market business, where it stood and the challenges it faced. Based on the overall situation presented, he then started to focus on his request to call down on his commitment as depicted below:

Oscar: Based on the current situation, I am considering calling down on my commitment.

Sean Kumar: What do you mean by calling down?

Oscar: I am confident of securing 1 new client, instead of 3.

Sean Kumar: You have a list of 30 qualified prospects in the system as far as your pipeline is concerned. And you have a track record of closing 1:8 the past years. I surely think that you are in the position to close 3 new clients based on the past track record, aren't you?

Oscar: I do have a list of 30 prospects in the system. However, based on my most recent review, only 50% of those prospects are qualified. In reality, I only have 15 qualified prospects at this point in time.

Sean Kumar: Hmmm. Are you telling me that the status of your prospects in the pipeline system is not up-to-date?

Oscar: Yes. I am afraid so. I am sorry for not being able to update it within time. However, here's the latest status of the qualified prospects, all 15 of them, which you can find in the presentation package Exhibit B.

Sean Kumar: <looking at Exhibit B> Ok. If you have 15 qualified prospects, why do you want to call down to 1 new client only?

Using the technique above, let's see how we can apply this:

Step 1: Gather the Information/Data

- Oscar is calling down his forecast from 3 to 1 client based on 50% reduction in his qualified prospect list from 30 to 15.
- Sean does not understand why Oscar can only close 1 out of the 15 considering that in the past Oscar had a closure rate of 1:8.

Step 2: Evaluate the Data

- Which data point is the most relevant to move the discussion to a positive route?

- Is the 50% reduction in the qualified prospect list the heart of the matter or the closure rate of 1:15?
- If the critical area is to still close 3 new clients, is it possible with only 15 qualified prospects? If it is, what would it take to achieve that?

Step 3: Give the Feedback

- **Purpose of the discussion:** To ensure that *Oscar keeps his commitment* of closing 3 new clients and the *behavior change* that you would like to see is that *Oscar should update the system regularly.*

- **Relevance of Data:** Apply the 4S (Specific, Significance, Seek to Understand, Suggestion) at this stage of thinking process:
  o **Specific:** Oscar's track record of 1:8 provides a good indicator of his chances of closing the deals as planned.
  o **Significance:** Oscar has the pipeline needed to close 3 new clients.
  o **Seek to understand**: Ask questions to find out why Oscar wanted to call down.
  o **Suggest**:
    - Encourage him based on his past track record, 15 qualified prospects is still good and ask him what assistance would he need to close 3 out of the 15.
    - Reinforce that regular updates in the system is essential if he wants to call down in the future else his commitment does not change.

- **'Fit to Purpose' Approach**: The business review session is a perfect fit for both timing and environment to give feedback. The most appropriate communication method is to have an in person discussion due to the seriousness of the discussion.

- **Prepare to give the feedback:**
  - Ensure that the information presented is valid. Keep to the specifics of the relevant data.
  - Adopt the appropriate behaviour of active engagement in a positive manner and in this scenario it is to appear firm and collaborative to find a solution to the problem.

Step 4: Conduct the feedback session.

Mid Year Review Feedback Engagement: Revised

Oscar: Based on the current situation, I am considering calling down on my commitment

Sean Kumar: *Please help me to understand what has changed since the last meeting.*

Oscar: I am confident of securing 1 new client, instead of 3 as the list of qualified prospects has reduced by 50% from 30 to 15.

Sean Kumar: *Based on the information that I have from the system, it still indicates 30 qualified prospects and therefore help me to understand where the difference is?*

Oscar: I am sorry but I have not been able to update the system.

Sean Kumar: *As you well know, we are all committed to our sales target based on what we have entered in the system. To not update the system at this stage is not acceptable as we are all accountable for the deliverables. Let's explore how we can increase the closure rate to 1:5 as we have to keep to our commitments.*

Can you identify the differences in the conversation? Do you think that the outcome of the discussion would be different?

Some of the differences are:

- Sean has taken a position of seeking to understand why Oscar is calling down on his commitment as oppose to taking a confrontational approach.
- Sean reiterates the importance of commitment and behavior that must be adhered to along with an offer to assist and help Oscar to meet his commitments.
- This is a more collaborative approach as oppose to accusatory.

How would you have structured the discussion? Try it out.

Example 2: Honing your Skills in a Performance Feedback Situation.

Based on the business review discussion above, we are going to use that as an example for Sean to give Oscar feedback around his performance.

Mid Year Review Feedback Engagement: Revised

Oscar: Based on the current situation, I am considering calling down on my commitment.

Sean Kumar: *Please help me to understand what has changed since the last meeting.*

Oscar: I am confident of securing 1 new client, instead of 3 as the list of qualified prospects has reduced by 50% from 30 to 15.

Sean Kumar: *Based on the information that I have from the system, it still indicates 30 qualified prospects and therefore help me to understand where the difference is?*

Oscar: I am sorry but I have not been able to update the system.

Sean Kumar: *As you well know, we are all committed to our sales target based on what we have entered in the system. To not update the system at this stage is not acceptable as we are all accountable for the deliverables. Let's explore how we can increase the closure rate to 1:5 as we have to keep to our commitments*

Step 1: Gather the Information/Data

- Oscar did not update the system and was not keeping to his commitment of sales closure

Step 2: Evaluate the Data

- Which data or behavior is more critical to reinforce or correct for performance review purposes? Is it his discipline in updating the system or the calling down on closure?
- Is there anything missing from the earlier discussion?

Step 3: Give the Feedback

- **Purpose of the discussion:** To correct behavior and to seek out other potential issues that might be affecting his performance.

- **Relevance of Data:** Apply the 4S (Specific, Significance, Seek to Understand, Suggestion) at this stage of thinking process:
  o **Specific:** Encourage him with recognition of his past performance (1:8 closure rates) and diligence in updating the system in the past.

- o **Significance:** Oscar has been a consistent performer and you would like him to continue to excel.
- o **Seek to understand**: Ask questions to find out why he does not have the confidence to achieve his commitments.
- o **Suggest**:
  - Encourage him based on his past performance he has the skills to achieve his goals.
  - Reinforce that regular updates in the system is essential as he is part of a team and everyone relies on one another.

Step 4: Conduct the feedback session.

Performance feedback session.

Sean Kumar: *Oscar, I was surprised the other day when you called down on your forecast from 3 to 1 as well as the reduction of the qualified prospects by 50%. You have been a consistent performer in the past with one of the better sales closure rate in the team and so I would like to take our session to understand what we can do together to ensure that the high level of performance is maintained.*

Oscar: I am sorry about that, I am not happy with what happened as well as and I think that it's due to the sudden change in the economic situation that caused a lot of the qualified prospect to delay their purchases but more significantly I was not able to determine the extent of that impact.

Sean Kumar: *Let me see if I am getting the issues correct, the challenge that you are facing is how to respond to the impact the economic situation is having on our business. Is that right?*

Oscar: Yes, that's correct. Plus I did not know what your reaction would be and I was concerned that I could have been fired.

Sean Kumar: *As you well know, we are all in this together as a team and I want to encourage you to ask me or the team for help when you need to as everyone is facing the same challenge. We rely on one another and therefore as soon as you have changes to be made, it must be made in the system so that it can be seen by everyone and as a team we can respond to the challenge. I know that it is challenging. What can I do to help you?*

It is important in a performance review to remember the following:

- Focus on behavior that needs to be reinforced or corrected for future performance improvements. Therefore, turn the attention away from sales or business review data point to behavior that contributes or lead up to the results will be helpful in the discussion. Note that Sean focused on issues related to Oscar's behavior and concerns rather than on the sales forecast or economic situation but used those points to reinforce the positive message of working together as a team and why it's critical to update the system.
- Relate your understanding and appreciation of the situation and its difficulties by summarising what you have heard is a good way of demonstrating that you are trying to understand the core issues.
- Recommend a suggestion or solution to the challenge.

How would you have conducted the review? Think about a past performance review and list down what you would have done differently.

Receiving Feedback

> **EAR**
> - **Engage** in the discussion by actively listening to what is being shared and be open and not defensive.
> - **Ask** clarifying questions and gather more information so that you are able to understand the intent and the desired change.
> - **Ready with** the action plan if necessary.

Example for Receiving Feedback

Let's practice receiving feedback using the examples from the previous chapter and assess how Oscar managed the discussion as well as how he might respond to the feedback.

Feedback Engagement for Employee Engagement Improvement

Oscar:	Good afternoon everyone. Thanks for making time to meet up today. My objective today is to seek feedback from all of you on your learning and development plan and career advancement opportunities. Three things that I want to find out are first, your views on the current learning and development plan, second, your views on career advancement opportunities and third, what do you want to see implemented this financial year within these two areas.
Emma:	Wow! That's interesting. I appreciate your openness in seeking our views in such a transparent manner.
David:	I feel the same way. And as far as I am concerned, I am having difficulty in assessing the kind of learning or skill sets training that I need to choose every year. What we have today is quite generic. I want something more tailored to my role.

Megan: I agree with David. I think it would be great if we have a role based competency roadmap. Then, all I need to do is select from the list of learning and development plan required for my role and competency.

John: In addition, I think it would be good also for us to discuss further on the unique development scope that we aspire during our 1:1 meeting with you. For example, I may want to explore being a project leader. We want the comfort feel that you are open to listening to our aspirations.

Oscar's role:

- **Engage** in the discussion. Listen to what is being said and list down the areas of discussion for example:

  o David has difficulty in accessing the kind of learning or skills set training as it is generic and he needs something more tailored to his role.

  o Megan expanded on the idea from David by suggesting that there should be a list of learning and development plan based on roles and competencies.

- **Ask** clarifying question to further understand the feedback and the desired improvement
- **Ready with** a plan.

So let's complete the example above with Oscar's reply to David and Megan's feedback. Let's observe what Oscar did:

Feedback Engagement for Employee Engagement Improvement Continued

Oscar: *Thank you for the feedback. Let me summarise what I have heard to ensure that I have the right level of understanding of the suggestion. David and Megan, both of you are suggesting that we should have development plans that are tailored by roles and competencies. Is that right?*

David: Yes that's correct.

Oscar: *David or Megan, can you please share more about the idea in terms of what you would expect to see and number of training courses or plans that you would be comfortable to do?*

Megan: I think that a list of not more than 3 training plans would be ideal as it would not consume too much of our time and a good balance between learning and still meeting our work goals.

David: Yeah, I agree.

Emma: Yes I think that's reasonable.

Oscar: *Thank you and based on David's feedback earlier, we can discuss further in our next one on one discussion and build a plan around it.*

Oscar demonstrated that:

- He was open to the feedback that he received, he was attentive and summarised to the team what he heard.
- He probed for greater clarity in the feedback as well as to get consensus and next steps.
- He moved to the next step with a simple action plan of discussing it further during a one on one session with the feedback as the basis of the plan.

Note what Oscar did not do:

- He was not defensive and did not push away the feedback.
- He did not push his idea across his team, he listened.

SECTION 5:

Moving Forward

9 So What's Next?

"You are the change you want in this world."
—Mahatma Gandhi

Tiger Woods. Roger Federer. Usain Bolt.

It is about being a champion. It is about being the best in your craft.

At this juncture, visualize yourself to be the best manager.

Be aware that feedback plays a vital role in improving your skills to master your craft.

Improvement can only happen when you do the following reiteratively:

- Step 1: Receive feedback in a constructive manner.
- Step 2: Decide on a call to action that reinforces specific behavioural change.
- Step 3: Act on it.
- Step 4: Check on progress.
- Step 5: Seek for feedback.
- Step 6: Go back to Step 1 (follow the same process again).

The diagram below depicts such process to achieve continuous improvement:

Feedback for Continuous Improvement

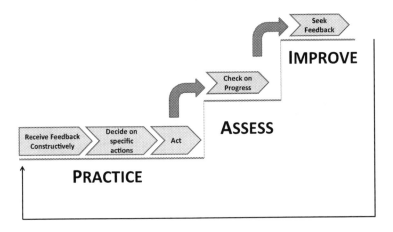

Let's walk through the process of 'Feedback for Continuous Improvement' and see how it works. As an example, let us use the Employee Engagement case study (Scenario 7.1.5) and go through the process step-by-step.

Step 1: Receive Feedback Constructively

A snapshot of the feedback that Oscar received is listed below:

Oscar: Great. I am just excited with all your enthusiasm and excellent feedback. All of you have recommended that we establish role-based learning and development plan to enable you to have a clear roadmap on the type of competency training that you need for the whole year. Since career advancement goes hand-in-hand with the learning and development plan, you have agreed that we treat this as a discussion that we will have during our 1:1 meeting session. We anticipate such discussion to happen either once or twice a year. We are taking a phased approach and will continue to improve the system and process as we go along. Did I capture everything that we have agreed?

Step 2: Decide on Specific Actions

Here is one of the lists of action items that Oscar decides to execute:

1) To establish role-based learning and development plan:

   a. Determine key competencies required for each role, in partnership with the HR Department. Estimated timeframe: 2 weeks.

   b. Determine competency-based training plan, whether to contract third party vendor or to develop in-house by the training department, in partnership with the HR Department. Estimated timeframe: 3 weeks.

   c. Develop role-based learning and development roadmap for each role, in partnership with HR. Estimated timeframe: 3 weeks.

   d. Develop learning platform infrastructure to enable self-paced on line training, in partnership with the IT team. Estimated timeframe: 4 weeks.

   e. Pilot the role-based learning and development plan. Estimated timeframe: 12 weeks.

Step 3: Act

Here are the sample action items that Oscar executes.

---

a. Determine key competencies required for each role, in partnership with the HR Department. Estimated timeframe: 2 weeks.

 a. List down all the relevant roles in his department.
 b. Validate each role against job descriptions and outcome expected.
 c. Refer to competency based model as provided by HR.
 d. Define all the required competences for each role
 e. Finalise with HR.

Step 4: Check on Progress

Let us assume that Oscar is now in the 12 week pilot implementation phase of the role-based learning and development plan. The scope of the pilot initially covered his four resources with a selection of one competency each. The success of the pilot is measured on the following variables:

- Completeness of the learning and development plan for my role.
- Ease of use.
- Relevancy of content.

Pilot users need to update a 'Pilot Progress Document' to Oscar on a weekly basis. The documents enlist the following, for instance:

Description	Acceptance Criteria	Pilot User 1 John	Pilot User 2 David	Pilot User 3 Megan	Pilot User 4 Emma
Completeness of the learning and development plan for my role	Clear roadmap on the learning plan and level of competency required for my role.	Yes	Yes	Yes	Yes
Ease of use	I can navigate easily from the learning menu to making selection on learning plan, booking learning time and taking learning exams.	Yes	Yes	Yes	Yes
Relevancy of content	I can apply what I learn in my work right away.	Yes	No. Content not available	No. Content not available.	No. Content not available.

Step 5: Seek for Feedback

At this stage, you have to adopt a critical view and explore specific areas for improvement. Ask clarifying and probing questions to ensure that you have a list of specific actions to execute upon.

In Oscar's example, based on the 'Pilot Progress Document', he seeks further feedback from his pilot users during the Pilot Progress Update Meeting, which is scheduled once every fortnight.

An example of the feedback session is listed below:

Oscar:	Thank you for updating the Pilot Progress Document. I appreciate your effort. Based on your feedback, there is one critical issue. Majority of you found that the content of the learning and development plan is not relevant due to the unavailability of the content. Tell me exactly what your experience was.
David:	I tried to access my learning content on Persuasive Communication for Competency Level 4; the content was not there.
Emma:	Yes. I experienced the same thing. Currently, the available content on Persuasive Communication is from Competency Level 1, 2 and 3 only. I was looking for Competency Level 4, and I experienced the same as David.
Megan:	I tried to access two other learning plans—Strategic Thinking Level 4 and Negotiation Skills Level 4. I experienced the same thing. I believe that the current learning and development plan only cater up to Level 3.
John:	I have no problems accessing any of my learning plans required for this year. Some of those are Level 4s as well. The two Level 4s that I took were Problem Solving Skills and Handling Difficult Conversations.

Oscar: Two possible situations are (1) some of the content is still under development (2) content is ready but not uploaded and tested yet. Since we have another 20 minutes or so for this meeting, can you all quickly review and list out the content that are not there yet please? I would like to take the full list and escalate it right away to our IT team.

All: Sure. I will do it right away.

Step 6: Go Back to Step 1 (follow the same process again)

Do the same process all over again.

Key Ideas for So, What's Next?

Continuous improvement is achieved when you perform these reiteratively:

- Receive feedback constructively.
- Decide on specific actions.
- Act on the feedback.
- Monitor progress.
- Seek further feedback.

---

10 Feedback Toolkit

> *"We first make our habits, and then our habits make us"*
>
> *—John Dryden*

The Feedback Toolkit is a simple system that helps you to effectively strive for continuous improvement by unleashing the power of feedback. It is designed with these in mind:

- The focus is about you.
- Cite small achievable goal on a weekly basis.
- Proactive approach in that you are not only capturing feedback that is given to you, but also seeking for feedback in specific areas and contributing to the organisation's continuous improvement by giving feedback to others.

There are two sections to the Feedback Toolkit, namely:

- Section 1: Weekly Feedback Details
    o Describes your weekly continuous improvement goal and the relevant feedback, observations and action items that you will follow through.

- Section 2: Monthly Progress Summary
  - o Describes the behavioural description, observations, action items and the weekly progress summary of improvement.

Table 10.1 below depicts the Feedback Toolkit template:

SECTION 1

GENERAL INFORMATION

Name:	
Division / Department:	
Company:	
Week of:	
Continuous Improvement Goal(s):	

FEEDBACK DETAILS

Behavioral description	Feedback Sought	Feedback Given	Feedback Received	Observations	Action Items

SECTION 2

MONTHLY PROGRESS SUMMARY

Behavioral Description	Observations	Action Items	Week 1	Week 2	Week 3	Week 4

How to Use the Feedback Toolkit?

Imagine a buddy system!

Whenever you go diving, you have to have a buddy (or a partner) and both of you have to look out for the safety of each other. You go down into the water with full commitment and conviction to each other. You agree on specific signals, conditions, rules and regulations for the safety of each other.

In the same manner, visualise you have a buddy who partners with you in your pursuit to perform your best in any endeavour that you undertake. The buddy oversees any areas that you can improve on. You are mentally prepared and readily accept your buddy's feedback because both of you have the same mission and goal—to be the best in your craft. Just like diving, you are committed to follow through your buddy's feedback because of your reliance on him or her in ensuring that you would continuously improve over time.

This is exactly how you should treat the Feedback Toolkit: It is your buddy!

Feedback Toolkit Guidelines:

The guidelines to use the Feedback Toolkit are listed below:

- Section 1:

    o General Information:
        - Fill out your name, division / department, company name, specific week and your continuous improvement goal(s).

    o Feedback Details:
        - Under the column behavioural description, write down the relevant behaviour which can be either one of the following:

- A specific behaviour that you intend to improve on.
- A feedback on behaviour that you give to others.
- A feedback on behaviour that you received from others.

- Mark (√), as applicable, in either one of the columns of:
  - Feedback sought when you intentionally seek for a specific feedback from others.
  - Feedback given when you intentionally give feedback to others.
  - Feedback received when you receive feedback from others.

- Under the observations column, list downs the detailed observations of a specific behaviour that the feedback applies to.

- Under the action items column, write down the action items that you decide to execute.

- Section 2:

  o Monthly Progress Summary:

    - Behavioural Description:
      - Capture the same behavioural description as Section 1.

    - Observations:
      - Capture the same observations as Section 1.

    - Action items:
      - Capture the same action items as Section 1.

- Week 1, Week 2, Week 3, Week 4 columns:
  - Capture progress that you achieve each week on the listed behaviour.

The emphasis of monitoring progress over a four week or one month period is based on the assumption that new behaviour can be adopted if you keep on doing it for at least 21 days. In the event that you still do not achieve the desired improvement within four weeks, then you can capture the same information again onto a new sheet and keep on monitoring it on a weekly basis until you achieve the desired improvement.

Appendix: Feedback Toolkit

Here is a sample of how Oscar uses the Feedback Toolkit during the month of July 2013.

SECTION 1

GENERAL INFORMATION

Name:	Oscar Lee
Division / Department:	Mid-Market Department
Company:	Innovative Solutions
Week of:	July 1st, 2013
Continuous Improvement Goal(s):	To secure buy-ins from team members on the introduction of a new KPI: 1) to sell internal consultancy (instead of just Partner's services) services together with the CRM implementation.

FEEDBACK DETAILS

Behavioural Description	Feedback Sought	Feedback Given	Feedback Received	Observations	Action Items
Communicate persuasively on the benefits of selling internal consultancy services			√ (from Sean Kumar)	"You quoted expensive service rates of internal consultants without demonstrating why they are better."	To design a unique service value proposition.
					Demonstrate why internal consultants are better—use Happy Insurance implementation example.

SECTION 2

MONTHLY PROGRESS SUMMARY

Behavioural Description	Observations	Action Items	Week 1	Week 2	Week 3	Week 4
		To design a unique service value proposition.	Communicate 1:1 with team member.	Revisit the same during 1:1 meeting with team member.	Discuss the same during the staff meeting.	Announce new KPI as planned.
Communicate persuasively on the benefits of selling internal consultancy services	"You quoted expensive service rates of internal consultants without demonstrating why they are better."	Demonstrate why internal consultants are better— use Happy Insurance implementation example.	Assess acceptance—2 out of 4 are comfortable. Need to work on the other 2.	Answer all questions and concerns.	Three seem good. One is still not biting.	Provide on-going advice and consultation to address concerns of the KPI implementation.
				1 person is still not comfortable.	Answer all questions and address all concerns	

Bibliography

Andersen, Erika, "I Love Jet Blue—Customer Service Done Right." Forbes.com, http://www.forbes.com/sites/erikaandersen/2012/03/19/i-love-jetblue-customer-service-done-right/

Customer Insight, "What is 360 degree feedback?" http://www.custominsight.com/360-degree-feedback/what-is-360-degree-feedback.asp

Drucker, Peter. *People and Performance: The Best of Peter Drucker on Management.* Harper's College Press, 1977.

Folkman, Joe and Dalton, Gene. *Turning Feedback into Change.* Provo, UT: Novations Group, 1996

Harris, Jamie O. *Giving Feedback.* Harvard Business School Press. 2006.

Hathaway, Patti. *Giving and Receiving Feedback; Building Constructive Communication.* Menlo Park, CA. Crisp Publications, 1998.

Honisch, Marty. "How to Analyze Survey Results (without getting in the weeds)." *Next Generation Consulting*, April 3rd, 2009.

Kelley, Brent. "What is Tiger Woods' Workout Routine?" About.com Blog, http://golf.about.com/od/tigerwoods/f/tiger-woods-workout.htm

Kelley, Brent. "How Much Does Tiger Woods Practice Golf?" About.com Blog, http://golf.about.com/od/tigerwoods/f/tiger-woods-practice.htm

Peiperl, Maury A. "Getting 360-Degree Feedback Right." Harvard Business Review, January—February 2001.

Mola, Michaela. "10 Key Things to Consider When Designing Surveys." Surveygizmo Blog, http://www.surveygizmo.com/survey-blog/designing-surveys/.

Sportsmail Reporter. "Need more chicken nuggets, Usain? Bolt claims lack of food led to slow race." *MailOnline*, May 29th, 2012.

Survey Monkey. "Smart Survey Design." http://s3.amazonaws.com/Survey MonkeyFiles/SmartSurvey.pdf

University of Wisconsin—Madison, "Survey Fundamentals: A Guide to Designing and Implementing Surveys." http://oqi.wisc.edu/resourcelibrary/uploads/resources/Survey%20Guide%20v%202.0.pdf

Welch, Jack with Welch, Suzy. *Winning.* New York: Harper, 2007

Zinser, Lynn. "Pushback on Nike Ad Celebrating Woods." *The New York Times,* March 26th, 2013.

About the Authors

Salwana Ali, Managing Director of Salwana and Rahim Associates Sdn Bhd, helps organizations improve performance. She consults on development of managers, organizational performance measures and improvement of business processes. Prior to founding her firm, she spent ten years in Microsoft leading and managing the public sector and enterprise business in Malaysia.

Lisa Lam enjoys the "learning" journey. She spent 20 years in the field of marketing, business operations and management. She has the unique experience of balancing the diverse Asian culture with the result oriented and direct approach of a Multinational organization, having worked at Microsoft in various countries in Asia (Malaysia, Singapore, and Thailand).